The
Healing Power
of the
Eucharist

The
Healing Power
of the
Eucharist

John Hampsch, C.M.F.

PUBLISHED BY ST. ANTHONY MESSENGER PRESS
CINCINNATI, OHIO

Cover design: Alicia Vazquez

LIBRARY OF CONGRESS CATALOGING-IN-PUBLICATION DATA

Hampsch, John H.
  The healing power of the Eucharist / John Hampsch.
    p.   cm.
  ISBN 1-56955-095-6 (alk. paper)
  1. Lord's Supper—Catholic Church.   2. Spiritual healing.   I. Title.
BX2215.2.H36   1999
234'.163—dc21   99-16841
                                                 CIP

ISBN-10: 1-56955-095-6
ISBN-13: 978-1-56955-095-3

Published by Servant Books, an imprint of
St. Anthony Messenger Press
28 W. Liberty St.
Cincinnati, OH 45202
www.ServantBooks.org

Printed in the United States of America

        09 10 11 12 15 14 13 12 11

Contents

A Close Encounter of the Preferred Kind

Imagine a person with a brain tumor asking a neurosurgeon to treat the disorder merely by giving medical advice over the telephone. Without a hands-on examination and a delicate, close-up surgical procedure, such long-distance "treatment" would be even more tragic than ludicrous.

In ordinary circumstances, physicians must be physically "present" with their patients to exercise their curative skills. Likewise, Jesus, the Divine Healer, seeks to be present with us, especially in exercising his *charism* of healing. It is true that when Jesus walked among us on earth, he could heal the sick from a distance, as he did the centurion's servant (see Matthew 8:5-13). But this was by exception. Ordinarily, Jesus' healing ministry was by "office call" (street encounter) or "house call" (as when he healed Peter's mother-in-law in Matthew 8:14-15). Thus a "close encounter" was the preferred kind. Being physically present to the patient was Jesus' usual *modus operandi* when healing, a ministry that accounted for two-thirds of his recorded miracles.

There is no closer encounter than a mutual, coactive, and intimate union called Communion. Certainly any coactivity of creature and Creator is truly awesome, but in the eucharistic encounter such intercommuning becomes eminently sacrosanct. In Holy Communion our body ingests and assimilates the sacramental elements that comprise Jesus' own physical body, while he in turn assimilates us into his very self. Using the meaningful word "abide" (*meno* in Greek), Jesus, with deft simplicity, describes this marvelous commingling presence for us in Scripture: "Whoever eats my flesh and drinks my blood *abides in me and I in him*" (Jn 6:56, RSV, emphasis added).

It is in this intimate contact, or touch, that Jesus most efficaciously releases his divine healing power. "Someone touched me...," Jesus exclaimed as a hemorrhaging woman was healed by a surreptitious touch of his garment, "I know that power has gone out from me," he said (Lk 8:46). Then he complimented the woman on her faith that triggered the release of that healing power.

Yet, besides this "contactual" presence that brings an intimate, physical, sacramental union with Christ in which he is "most especially present" (*Catechism of the Catholic Church*, 373), there are other forms of Christ's presence. As the Church has affirmed, "The faithful share in it [the Mass] both *spiritually*, by faith and charity, and *sacramentally*, through the banquet of Holy Communion" (*Eucharisticum Mysterium*, May 25, 1967). Thus, the unity of believers with each other in one body or assembly is both brought about and expressed in the sacrament of the eucharistic bread (see 1 Corinthians 10:17), and Vatican II tells us that all persons are called to this unity, *in union with Christ* (*Lumen Gentium*, 3). By sharing the broken bread, Christ, "they enter into communion with him and form but one body with him" (*Catechism of the Catholic Church*, 1329).

This corporate or "communitarian" (spiritual) presence of

Christ in the liturgical assembly was the first meaning of the phrase "communion of saints" as used in the Apostles' Creed. And like Christ's physical presence in the actual receiving of Holy Communion, his communitarian presence carried with it its own unique form of healing "touch."

Thus, a multiform encounter with Christ occurs within the framework of the eucharistic liturgy, which Vatican II reminds us is "the summit toward which the activity of the Church is directed,... the fount from which all her power flows" (*Constitution on the Sacred Liturgy,* 10).

One form of that power is healing power, as recognized from the first century, for St. Ignatius of Antioch referred to it as "the *medicine* of immortality." But, amazingly, in spite of its availability, pitifully few people ever seek healing in the context of the Holy Eucharist. It is precisely because this multifaceted gift of God's healing power in the Eucharist is neglected by the vast majority of those who claim to know Christ that this book is written. This volume is an enhanced explanation of what I have referred to in one of my other books, *Healing Your Family Tree,* as "the most powerful means of healing known to man."

A special word of tribute and appreciation is due to Gary Seromik for applying his fine editing skills to the arduous task of bringing this work to completion. The material from which he worked was a motley collection of manuscripts of mine, several audiotapes of talks I have given, and a raft of desultory notes I have collected over the years. To assemble these into a unified manuscript for publication was no mean task. For his dedication to this work I am sincerely grateful.

I would like to invite each reader to pray that Jesus may draw countless souls to himself to experience the joy of his compassionate healing love that flows from his Eucharistic Heart, and that Our Lady of the Eucharist, without whom we would not have the Body of Christ to receive, may intercede for us, her spiritual children, for all our needs from her divine Son.

John H. Hampsch, C.M.F.
Claretian Tape Ministry
P.O. Box 19100
Los Angeles, CA 90019-0100

The Power of Grace

At the Lawrence Livermore Laboratory in Berkeley, California, scientists have been working on a "Shiva," a machine designed to produce nuclear fission by focusing many laser beams onto a pellet of hydrogen isotopes about the size of a period. The concentrated lasers can induce fission of the subatomic particles, thereby releasing a burst of enormous energy. This energy is the same type that makes the sun and the stars shine for countless centuries.

In fact, one scientist has calculated that if the total energy contained in one gram of matter were released, it would be sufficient to lift a one-million-ton object six miles into the air! For those who are not well-versed in science, it is startling to learn that this energy resides in prodigious quantities in every gram of matter. As many of the current sources of energy are being depleted rapidly, such a hidden source of energy is a potential gold mine. Indeed, the challenge that modern science now faces is finding a practical way to release and direct this stored energy, and many of the efforts of our modern technological age are directed to this very purpose.

At some point every high school student learns in science class that potential energy must be released as kinetic or actualized energy before it can produce any physical change or motion. This principle applies to all twelve types of known energy in the universe (gravitational, thermal, electromagnetic, nuclear, chemical, and so on). All these forms of energy are potential—and useless—until they are actualized. For instance, the gravitational energy in the water behind a dam is useless until the water is released; only then does the gravity of the falling water turn the wheels of the turbines that produce electricity. Likewise, the chemical energy in gasoline has to be released as kinetic energy by a spark igniting the gasoline vapor in the engine's piston chambers, thereby providing the energy needed to turn the wheels of the car and make it work.

This same basic principle of potential energy becoming kinetic or actual energy has a parallel in the spiritual arena. Like the gargantuan energies hidden in every gram of matter, enormous spiritual energies lie hidden and untapped all around us. We are surrounded by enormous amounts of grace, which, if tapped into and used in even the smallest amount, could transform our lives and our eternity. Tapping into grace transforms our potential sanctification into actual sanctification. Indeed, the enormous spiritual energies hidden around us are more numerous than the natural energies available in nature.

How do we receive grace? There are three major avenues for receiving grace. First of all, we can receive grace through some form of prayer: prayer of blessing and adoration, prayer of petition, intercessory prayer, prayer of thanksgiving, or prayer of praise. Likewise, it can be any expression of prayer: vocal prayer, meditation, contemplative prayer, community prayer, liturgical prayer, psalm prayer, or Scripture prayer. They all confer grace so that we are holier after praying than we were before we started praying.

The second major source of that spiritual energy we call

grace comes from practicing the virtues, such as faith, hope, charity, prudence, justice, fortitude, and temperance. In fact, some fifty-six virtues have been catalogued over the years. (Even suffering could be considered a virtue when it is motivated by love, since it could be a manifestation of the virtues of fortitude, perseverance, mortification, temperance, and self-control.)

The third source of grace is the seven sacraments. Three of the seven sacraments—baptism, confirmation, and holy orders—can be received only once during a person's lifetime. They confer a sacramental seal by which a person shares in Christ's priesthood and is made a member of the church. This seal is indelible; it remains always with the person as a promise and guarantee of divine protection.

Two other sacraments are received infrequently. Matrimony is generally received only once, although in some cases, such as remarriage after the death of a spouse, the sacrament may be repeated. The anointing of the sick is administered whenever a person is in danger of death from sickness or old age. It may be repeated when there is a change in the severity of the condition or when the person suffers some relapse after a recovery. In general, though, the majority of Christians will not receive this sacrament with any frequency.

Of the seven sacraments, only two—the sacraments of reconciliation (penance) and the Eucharist—may be received frequently. And of the seven, the Eucharist is the greatest source of grace. When we receive the Eucharist we receive not only grace but the very Author of Grace; in receiving the Eucharist we do not receive a *thing,* but God himself in his human nature as Christ and his divine nature as God. Consequently, the Eucharist transcends any other source of grace, and as St. Thomas Aquinas asserts, it is the ultimate focal point of all the other sacraments.

We can attain great holiness by prayer alone. We can also attain advanced holiness by practicing any one of the virtues, since the full spectrum of virtue grows, as St. Thomas Aquinas explains, the way the hand grows—not one finger at a time but all together. As one finger grows, the other fingers grow simultaneously. Likewise, as we practice any one virtue, the other virtues will grow too. But when it comes to maximizing our holiness, nothing exceeds the sacraments as a source of grace. The seven sacraments are designed by God to be the main avenues of our encounter with him, and among the sacraments, the Eucharist is the greatest in terms of conferring grace and having the power to make us holy.

Jesus instituted the Eucharist at the Last Supper, which was the first Mass. He consecrated the bread and the wine and said, "This is my body…. This is my blood," and mandated that this ritual be continued through the ages: "Do this in remembrance of me" (see Luke 22:19-20). The key element here is that receiving Jesus puts us in contact not just with grace but with the very Author of Grace in the re-enactment of his redemptive sacrifice, referred to in Hebrews 2:10 (NAB): "For it was fitting that he, for whom and through whom all things exist, in bringing many children to glory, should make the leader to their salvation perfect through suffering."

Any occasion of growth in holiness, such as the reception of a sacrament, must be sparked by grace *before* it can bring about actual growth in holiness and earn for us a heavenly reward. Just as the spark from the spark plug is needed to get the car moving, a spark is also needed to transform potential grace into actual grace, to transfer this life of God we call grace from God, the Creator, to us creatures, who are made in the image and likeness of God, and are thus amenable to receiving this grace. Theologians call this spark of grace *prevenient grace,* grace that prompts us to use grace. This concept is based on Philippians 2:13, where Paul says, "It is God who works in you, both to *will* and to *act* according to his good purpose" (emphasis added). In other words, God is there nudging you to acquiesce with the will in order to do something you had planned to do with the will. Although God does not touch the freedom of the will (you are still free to reject his work in you), he is the one who inspires you to respond in a positive way.

Hebrews 12:2 tells us that Jesus "is the author and perfecter of our faith." "Author" means the source; "perfecter" means the one who brings to completion or perfection. In the book of Revelation (21:6), Jesus speaks of himself as the Alpha and the Omega—the first and last letters of the Greek alphabet—signifying that he is the beginning and the end. He is the source or efficient cause, and the end or final purpose. To *will* and to *act.* Once we understand this divine dynamic and enter into any of the three avenues of grace—prayer, the virtues, or the sacraments—we will become more responsive to grace's awesome function in our lives.

ONE

The Transforming Power of the Eucharist

G od's grace is available to us when we participate in the eucharistic liturgy as part of the Mystical Body of Christ, but especially when we, as part of the Mystical Body, are nourished by Christ's physical body in the premiere sacrament of the Eucharist. The eucharistic presence of Jesus has the power to transform us: there is tremendous potential energy waiting to be released in the consecrated host and the consecrated wine that we receive in Communion. God himself initiated this source of grace and extends to us a pleading invitation to receive him in this sacrament. Subsequent sanctifying grace, which is holiness-making grace, will then flow into our souls by the special mutual union called *Communion* that occurs when we receive the Eucharist.

It is important for us to realize that the union that occurs in the Eucharist is a special, mutual union. This is why we commonly refer to the receiving of the Eucharist as *Communion*, meaning *union with.* Jesus is speaking to us about the mutuality of this union when he says, "He who eats my flesh and drinks my blood abides in me, and I in him" (Jn 6:56, RSV). Clearly he is speaking about a reciprocal action that occurs when we receive Communion. Jesus comes to us in this sacrament and acts in us. But his coming to us and acting in us should evoke some kind of response on our part. We have to abide in him.

As we respond to Jesus' pleading invitation to let him abide in us and let ourselves abide in him in Holy Communion, we are in a better position to release the potential power of this sacrament. As a result, marvelous things can happen to our souls, our bodies, and our minds. All the benefits of this union are accomplished within the context of the Lord's Supper, the ancient, revered name for the Mass, which today is often called the Celebration of the Eucharist.

We know that the Lord, in his providence, provides us with natural food to nourish and sustain our bodies. This physical food, which is necessary for life, gives us the energy or the power we need to stay alive, work, play, and think. If we did not eat, malnutrition would set in, our bodies would gradually deteriorate, and ultimately we would die of starvation.

Just as God provides us with food to sustain our physical or natural life, even more importantly he provides us with food to sustain our spiritual life. In John 6:27 Jesus says, "Do not work for food that spoils, but for food that endures to eternal life, which the Son of Man will give you." This remark is significant. Like so many of Jesus' remarks, it is an enigmatic phrase pregnant with deep theological content. The spiritual food that Jesus gives us will prevent us from ever growing hungry. We will never be spiritually undernourished: "I am the bread of life. He who comes to me will never go hungry, and he who believes in me will never be thirsty" (Jn 6:35). When we resolve to cooperate fully with God's design and allow the power of the Eucharist to be released in our lives, remarkable things can happen.

Unfortunately, most people do not respond appreciatively, that is, devotionally, in a faith-filled way. Jesus abides in us, but we do not really abide in him as we should. By not responding to the transforming power available in the Eucharist, we truncate the healing power that we would otherwise receive; we deprive ourselves of God's power and we obtund God's work within us.

Our resolve to cooperate fully with God's design in the release of this eucharistic power—especially its healing power—can bring about astonishing personal effects in our bodies and our minds. Moreover, the release of this eucharistic power can have world-changing effects. The Blessed Mother described these two effects, personal and global (or societal), during her alleged apparition in Medjugorje, Bosnia-Herzegovina, on September 25, 1995.* The visionaries reported the following message from Mary, one of those announced publicly on the 25th of each month:

Today I invite you to fall in love with Jesus in the most holy sacrament of the altar. Adore him in your parishes and in this way you will be united with the entire world. Jesus will become your friend and you will not talk of him like some-

---

*Although these apparitions are still being investigated by the Church at the time I am writing, many reputable theologians have studied the words Mary has given the visionaries and have not found anything in them contradictory to faith or morals. In fact, many people have been called to repentance and conversion upon hearing these words in all their simplicity.

one that you barely know. Unity with him will be a joy for you and you will become witnesses of the love of Jesus that he has for every creature. Little children, when you adore Jesus, you are also very close to me.

Let us look at Mary's words more closely and let them transform our hearts. Mary invites us "to fall in love with Jesus in the most holy sacrament of the altar." Here, of course, she is referring to Jesus in the Blessed Sacrament—the Eucharist. She encourages us to adore *him* (not *it*) in our parishes, so we "will be united with the entire world." She reminds us of the personal relationship of the sacrament while alluding to its global or societal effect, which unites us with believers around the world. Elaborating on the personal relationship, she emphasizes that Jesus will become our friend and he will be an *intimate* friend, not merely an acquaintance. Our unity—or union by Communion—with him will be a joy. We will become "witnesses of the love of Jesus that he has for every creature." Thus communion with Jesus does not have merely an *intra*personal effect; and significantly, it also has an *inter* personal effect.

When we adore Jesus in the Blessed Sacrament, he becomes our personal friend. Jesus told his apostles this truth at the Last Supper when he established the sacrament of the Eucharist: "I no longer call you servants, because a servant does not know his master's business. Instead, I have called you friends, for everything that I learned from my Father I have made known to you" (Jn 15:15). Jesus is telling us that the Eucharist is not only the premiere point of encounter for *communicating* with him but more significantly for *communing* with him. He becomes our friend in such a way that we no longer have a "dead" picture of him as a mere historical personality who lived two thousand years ago. We come to know him with real spiritual intimacy and have a feel for his personality, just as we would with any close personal friend. This is the kind of warm and existential intimacy Jesus wants us to cultivate—a spiritual intimacy which Mary says will be a "joy" for us.

Encountering Christ Personally

We should ask ourselves, "Has this been my experience? Do I experience an ever-deepening joy in intimacy with Christ? Do I have a real personal relationship with Jesus?" Our good Protestant friends, the evangelicals, rightly say we need to have a *personal relationship* with Jesus and receive him as our *personal* Savior. This is based on Galatians 2:20, where St. Paul says, "I live by faith in the Son of God, who loved me and gave himself for me." Notice that St. Paul does not say *us*, but *me*: "...who has loved *me* and gave himself for *me* (emphasis added)." St. Augustine once said, "God loves each of us and Jesus died for each one of us as if there were only one of us."

We should examine our consciences to see if we have this habitual, personalized relationship with Jesus. If we do, a far greater power will be released when we receive him in person in the Eucharist. The potential power present in the sacrament will be actualized. Potential energy will be transformed into kinetic energy. We will become more aware of his presence and his power within us.

Theologians speak of different forms in which we encounter Christ, all of which are mentioned in Scripture. For example, St. Paul, in Colossians 1 and Romans 8, speaks about the *omni-present* Christ, pervasive throughout all creation. The *altruistic* presence of Christ (finding Christ in our fellow human beings) is recorded in Matthew 25:40: "Amen, I say to you, whatever you did for one of these least brothers of mine, you did for me (NAB)." We find Christ in a community—the *communitarian* presence of Christ—in Matthew 18:20: "For where two or three are gathered together in my name, there am I in the midst of them (NAB)." But the *eucharistic* encounter is a special one. In the Eucharist, our encounter with Jesus is a physical one, not just a spiritual one.

All these forms of encounter with Christ are real. But only in the Eucharist is Christ both sacramentally and physically present. Therefore, receiving Christ in the Eucharist offers us the largest conduit of grace. As an illustration, both a ten-foot-wide pipe and a half-inch-wide pipe can convey water, but one can convey a greater amount than the other. So it is with the forms of encountering Christ. The one that conveys the greatest grace is the eucharistic encounter with Christ in Holy Communion.

The fact that this eucharistic encounter with Christ generally occurs within the context of the celebration of the Eucharist with other believers further enhances both the meaning and the power of the sacrament. The Eucharist is no longer a one-to-one encounter. It becomes the societal encounter *par excellence*, giving an even deeper meaning to Jesus' words in Matthew 18:20.

The author of the Letter to the Hebrews admonishes the

Jewish Christians with these words: "Let us not give up meeting together, as some are in the habit of doing, but let us encourage one another—and all the more as you see the Day approaching" (Heb 10:25). Why does the writer admonish the believers in this way? Because they are missing out on that *communitarian* presence of Christ. It is within this communitarian presence that they can have the personal, sacramental encounter with Jesus present in the Eucharist. That is why the early Christians "devoted themselves to the apostles' teaching and to the fellowship, to the breaking of bread and to prayer" (Acts 2:42). We will examine this dimension of the Eucharist more closely in a later chapter.

God's transforming power is available to us, therefore, both individually, as he transforms us through our personal relationship with him, and corporately, as the joy we share in him makes us more effective witnesses to others of his fathomless love. His healing power is not limited to just ourselves; it can have a broader effect that reaches through us to others, far more effectively than we might imagine.

TWO

Jesus, the Bread of Life

Among the ancient warring Anglo-Saxons, guarding the food supply was an important assignment. Since bread was the primary staple food at that time, this task essentially meant guarding the bread supply. Because the Anglo-Saxons constantly feared that the enemy would pilfer their food and cause starvation, someone was always responsible for guarding it.

It is worthwhile examining some etymology here. In early English, the person in charge of this critical assignment for the survival of the community was called a *halfweard*; this word referred to the trusted "loaf ward" or "loaf keeper" for the community. In time the term was contracted to *hlaford*. By the Middle Ages, the word had first evolved into *laferd* and then *loverd*. Finally, in later English, the word was reduced to the familiar word *lord*, and was the expression used to refer to the master of the household supplies, especially the bread supplies. The word was further ennobled as the English translation of the Latin word *dominus*. The root for this word is *domus*, meaning "household" or "house" in Latin. In Roman culture, the *dominus*, or lord, was a position of prestige related to controlling the household's food supply, the mainstay of which was bread.

It is certainly more providential than coincidental that Jesus acknowledged for himself the title *Lord*: "You call me 'Teacher' and 'Lord,' and rightly so, for that is what I am" (Jn 13:13). As we have already seen, etymologically the lord or "master of the household" was the keeper of the bread supply. Jesus referred to himself with the phrase "master of the household supplies" or "food provider," reflecting the origins of the word *lord* in the parable recorded in Matthew 24:45-51: "Who then is the faithful and wise servant, whom the master [of the household] has put in charge of the servants in his household to give them their food at the proper time?" (Mt 24:45). And he again appropriated this title for himself in Matthew 10:25: "If they have called the master of the house Beelzebul, how much more those of his household!" (NAB).

Upon further investigation, we uncover even more interesting little details that seem far from being coincidental. Was it coincidental that Jesus—this "master of the household," this "master of the food supplies"—was born in Bethlehem, which means *House of Bread*? Coincidental that Jesus, who would later call himself the Bread of Life, was laid as a newborn infant in a manger, a box designed to hold food for the livestock in the stable?

Jesus' public ministry is replete with instances where he points to God as the giver of such sustenance. When Jesus began his public ministry, his disciples asked him to teach them how to pray. In the prayer that he taught them, the Our Father, which is transmitted through Scripture to us today, he instructs us to ask the Father for "our daily bread" (i.e., our material needs).

In the course of his public ministry, Jesus exercised this office of master of the food supply in a tangible way on at least a couple of occasions, as recorded in the Gospels. On one occasion he miraculously multiplied five barley loaves the size of a fist to feed five thousand men (not counting the women and children), leaving twelve baskets of leftovers. Among the many miracles of Jesus, this one enjoyed the widest audience participation. In fact, this is the only miracle besides the Resurrection that is mentioned in all four Gospels, so it must have made an indelible impression on the minds of the four gospel writers. On yet another occasion he fed four thousand men with seven loaves.

But to admire the miracle without learning its lesson, St. Augustine says, is like admiring beautiful handwriting without knowing how to read. St. John had a special gift for conveying not only Jesus' words and deeds but also the lesson behind them. His account of this miracle in the sixth chapter of his Gospel is the point of departure for one of the most fascinating and profound passages in the New Testament—a teaching on the Eucharist.

As is often the case in Holy Scripture, when God intends to do something extraordinary, he prepares his people for it by revealing beforehand what he is about to do. Here, Jesus was about to tell the people that he intended to give them his Body and Blood as food for their souls. He was about to reveal to them the new and amazing doctrine of the real presence. So he prepared them for hearing this mysterious teaching by working a truly astounding miracle.

St. John situates this miracle at the time of the Jewish feast of the Passover. A large crowd was following Jesus, drawn by the fact that he was healing so many people. Jesus knew the people would be hungry. St. John tells us that Jesus already knew what he was going to do, but he decided to test his disciple, Philip, and asked him, "Where can we buy enough food for them to eat?" Poor Philip could not even begin to think of a way to feed such a crowd! He pointed out to Jesus that it would take two hundred days' wages to buy enough food to feed everyone even a minimal amount of food.

Suddenly, a small boy approached Jesus and his apostles, offering them five small barley loaves and two small fish. Certainly this meager offering appeared rather pitiful because even the apostle Andrew remarked, "What good are these for so many?" Nonetheless, Jesus had all the people recline so they could eat. We know what happened next: "Looking up to heaven, he said the blessing, broke the loaves, and gave them to the disciples, who in turn gave them to the crowds" (Mt 14:19, NAB). Everyone ate until they were satisfied. Jesus then instructed the disciples to collect the food that was left over. When they did, they had twelve baskets full of fragments from the five barley loaves. Having witnessed this miracle, the crowd was so awestruck they wanted to take Jesus by force and make him their king. However, Jesus perceived this and fled.

A Preview of the Eucharist

Undoubtedly, Jesus fed the people because they were hungry. But it also seems clear that this was an ideal opportunity to give his followers an image of the sacrament he would formally institute one year later at the Last Supper. How do we see the Eucharist prefigured in this miracle? The imagery is powerful and overwhelming!

First of all, the miracle takes place "as the Passover draws near," the same time of the year that Jesus would later choose to institute the Eucharist. The proximity of this feast certainly must have evoked images of Moses among the people in the crowd. As we shall see later, the Gospel writers capitalize on this imagery to portray Jesus as the new Moses. For example, Jesus ascended a mountain before feeding the people miraculous bread, just as Moses ascended a mountain before supplying the Israelites with manna as they wandered in the desert.

Second, Jesus uses the same sequence of actions here that he repeats at the Last Supper: he takes the bread, blesses it, and distributes it to his disciples, who in turn give it to the people.

Third, Jesus' blessing of the bread has supernatural power in both instances. In this case, the bread is miraculously multiplied to feed five thousand men. At the Last Supper, Jesus miraculously changes ordinary bread and wine into his Body and Blood.

Fourth, Jesus provides his followers with all the material sustenance they need at the miracle of the loaves and fishes. In fact, the gospels tell us the people ate until they were full, and an abundant surplus of twelve full baskets still remained. In the Eucharist, Jesus provides us with all the spiritual sustenance we need to live for him. We can receive the Eucharist fully expecting that Christ will give us spiritual life through it. Moreover, Christ is not stingy; his provision for us is abundant. Not only will he take care of our spiritual needs, but we can also trust he will take care of our material needs as well (metaphorically expressed in the phrase "our daily bread").

To escape the crowd, Jesus fled back to the mountain alone. That night he miraculously walked on the waters of the Sea of Galilee, frightening his disciples, who had rowed some three or four miles on the lake to Capernaum. By the following morning, the crowd had followed Jesus to Capernaum.

At this point, St. John launches into one of the most profound and spiritual passages in the New Testament. Realizing that the miracle of the loaves and fishes had made a big impression on the people, Jesus took advantage of this occasion to reveal the deeper spiritual truth behind what they had witnessed the day before. St. John recalls the promise which Christ made of the heavenly food he was about to give the world—the Eucharist.

Jesus was concerned that the crowd was following him for the wrong reason: "Amen, amen, I say to you, you are looking for me not because you saw signs but because you ate the loaves and were filled. Do not work for food that perishes but for the food that endures for eternal life, which the Son of Man will give you. For on him the Father, God, has set his seal" (Jn 6:26-27, NAB). Jesus chided the crowd for following him only because they were satisfied by the physical nourishment he provided, and told them that they should be looking beyond the food of this world to the spiritual bread that will give them eternal life. We too need to ask ourselves if we are following Jesus for himself or for what he can do for us.

Jesus' conversation with the crowd is reminiscent of Moses' experience with the Israelites in the desert. When they were without food, God sent them manna from heaven. But they overlooked God's miraculous provision and grumbled because they wanted more variety and something more tasty, like the food they had in Egypt. God was providing for them in a supernatural way, but they did not value his gift to them. They were more interested in satisfying their hunger than in the fact that God was revealing his glory. Just as the Israelites under Moses were oblivious to the deeper significance of the miracle of the manna, so too were their descendants, who failed to understand the significance of Jesus' words and miracles.

The crowd was curious: "What can we do to accomplish the works of God?" Jesus answered them forthrightly: "This is the work of God, that you believe in the one he sent" (Jn 6:29, NAB). Jesus was revealing to the crowd that they had to believe in his word before he could lead them deeper to the truth of the Eucharist, the Bread of Life. They had to open themselves up to God's grace and make an act of faith before their eyes would be open to the truth of his words.

Recalling how their ancestors ate bread from heaven during their years of wandering with Moses in the desert, the crowd asked Jesus, "What sign can you do?" that they might believe in him (v. 30, NAB). Jesus answered, "Amen, amen, I say to you, it was not Moses who gave the bread from heaven: my Father gives you the true bread from heaven. For the bread of God is that which comes down from heaven and gives life to the world" (Jn 6:32-33, NAB).

The Real Presence in the Eucharist

Their conversation had come to a crossroads. Who was greater? Moses or Jesus? Jesus did not avoid the issue but bluntly described himself as the Bread of Life, through whom a person may obtain eternal life and spiritual sustenance while still on earth: "I am the bread of life; whoever comes to me will never hunger, and whoever believes in me will never thirst" (Jn 6:35, NAB). As St. Augustine has observed, Jesus spoke of himself in a way that made him seem superior to Moses, for Moses never dared to say he would give food which would never perish but would endure to eternal life. Moses promised plenty of food for the belly, St. Augustine said, but the food Moses promised was food that perishes. Jesus, on the other hand, promised food which never perishes but which endures forever.

Needless to say, Jesus' words sent a stir through the crowd. Was this not Joseph's son, whose father and mother they knew so well? How could he say that he had come down from heaven? Was he not an ordinary human being just like them? How could he claim to be God? Yet, Jesus did not mitigate his words. Up until then, he had presented himself as the Bread of Life, faith in him was food for eternal life. Now Jesus challenged the crowd even further. "Amen, amen, I say to you, whoever believes has eternal life. I am the bread of life. Your ancestors ate the manna in the desert, but they died; this is the bread that comes down from heaven so one may eat it and not die. I am the living bread that came down from heaven; whoever eats this bread will live forever; and the bread that I will give is my flesh for the life of the world" (Jn 6:47-51, NAB). The nobility of this great gift of God to nourish and empower us was epitomized in Jesus' words, "The bread that I give is my flesh for the life of the world."

By this time, the people in the crowd were quarreling among themselves. "How can this man give us his flesh to eat?" they asked. They certainly must have found the idea repulsive since it smacked of cannibalism. Jesus' response was to further elaborate on his teaching: "Amen, amen, I say to you, unless you eat the flesh of the Son of Man and drink his blood, you do not have life within you. Whoever eats my flesh and drinks my blood has eternal life and I will raise him on the last day. For my flesh is true food, and my blood is true drink. Whoever eats my flesh and drinks my blood remains in me and I in him. Just as the living Father sent me and I have life because of the Father, so also the one who feeds on me will have life because of me. This is the bread that came down from heaven. Unlike your ancestors who ate and still died, whoever eats this bread will live forever" (Jn 6:53-58, NAB).

This passage is, in essence, the culminating point of Jesus' conversation with the crowd. Jesus was speaking extremely harsh words to them, seemingly asking them to be like cannibals. Once again, he did not attempt to disguise his words. Scripture scholars point out that the word "eat" used in most translations of this passage is rather neutral in meaning compared to the Greek word that was used in ancient manuscripts of this Gospel. The true meaning of the Greek word is better conveyed by English words such as "gnaw," "munch," "masticate," and "feed upon." In fact, the Greek verb is normally used to describe animals as they eat.

As we read this chapter, we cannot fail to notice that the crowd was growing progressively antagonistic to the words Jesus was speaking. By this time, it is quite clear that most of the people in the crowd, especially those who were there out of curiosity or hoping for more food, could not accept what Jesus was telling them. Verse 41 tells us that the people were "murmuring" about Jesus. By verse 52, they are "quarreling" among themselves.

But this reaction was not limited just to the general audience. Even Jesus' disciples, those who were following him because they believed in him until now, were scandalized by Jesus' words to them and could not accept them. In verse 60, St. John recalls their reaction: "This saying is hard; who can accept it?" In the following verse, they too were "murmuring" about this teaching. At this point, Jesus confronted his disciples head-on: "Does this shock you?" he asked. Here we need to note that Jesus did not make any effort to compromise his teaching. He did not attempt to tell the people they were mistaken or they did not really understand what he was saying. He tested their faith to the limit by not "theologizing" the fact that by consuming his *entire living body* with his soul and divinity as a *full person,* they would be assimilating his complete personhood. Consequently, in verse 66, we learn that "many of his disciples returned to their former way of life and no longer accompanied him."

Jesus challenged both the curious onlookers in the crowd and his own disciples. Many were disillusioned and left him because he refused to compromise his teaching. They were, in a sense, like so many people today who want a theological explanation or scientific proof of a teaching. They were weak in faith. They were skeptics, not prepared to accept anything on faith. Most of those who walked away from Jesus had already shown some commitment to him. Just as their faith in Jesus was weak, so too was their love for him.

Even though many of Jesus' disciples abandoned him at this point, the twelve apostles did not. They had come to know Jesus intimately and to believe in him. Still, Jesus challenged them: "Do you also want to leave?" (v. 67). Speaking on behalf of the others, Peter answered, "Master, to whom shall we go? You have the words of eternal life. We have come to believe and are convinced you are the Holy One of God" (Jn 6:68-69, NAB). The noble simplicity of the apostles' faith is a shining example for all of us. They did not hesitate to believe Jesus' words to them. Furthermore, they accepted his words at face value, fully embracing and believing his promise to give them his real flesh to eat and his real blood to drink. They believed in faith because, as Peter said, he was "the Holy One of God." From this point on, they were expecting that Jesus would fulfill his promise.

St. John ends this chapter on a note that intimately links it to the gospel accounts of the Last Supper. Alluding to Judas' eventual betrayal, Jesus prophetically asks, "Did I not choose twelve? Yet is not one of you a devil?" (Jn 6:70).

At the appointed time a year later at the Last Supper, everyone, with the exception of Judas, was prepared. When Jesus took the loaf of bread and the cup of wine, blessed them and gave thanks, and gave them to his disciples saying, "Take and eat; this is my body," and, "Drink from it, all of you, for this is my blood of the covenant, which will be shed on behalf of many for the forgiveness of sins" (Mt 26:26-27, NAB), the disciples knew exactly what Jesus was doing. They knew too exactly who Jesus was. They knew the bread was changed into his true flesh, and the wine was changed into his true blood. Their belief in the real presence of Jesus in the Eucharist was firm.

From the beginning of his life on earth, Jesus wanted it to be known that one of his main functions was to give us sustenance for life. Everything about him—from the place he was born to the prayer he taught us, the miracles he performed, and his teachings to us—coalesce to show us he is the Master of the household bread supply. He is the Lord. He is the Food-Provider. His whole mission is to sustain us unto eternal life. About one year before Holy Thursday, when he instituted the sacrament of the Eucharist at the Last Supper on the night before he died, he was already prophesying that he would cata-pult us into eternal life through the redemptive act of Calvary, and that, a few hours before doing so, he would consecrate the bread that was his very flesh to sustain us here on earth. The last act of his life on earth before his death was in itself a kind of "preview" of that sacrificial, redemptive act, for that body "given" would also be "given up". Similarly, his blood, which would be shed the following day "on behalf of many," was pre-sented at the last supper as the "cup of salvation." (Ps 116:13)

If we gather all the elements of Jesus' teachings in the gospels so we have a global perspective, everything leads to this climac-tic point of salvation history. Jesus is telling us something very basic. As ordinary bread sustains our natural life, Jesus is the Bread of Life that sustains our eternal life. For this reason, the

Catholic Church for twenty centuries has never ceased to have the Holy Sacrifice of the Mass as its central liturgical act, during which the Eucharist is ultimately confected. Nonetheless, audience participation is as much a part of the eucharistic miracle today as it was of the miracle of the multiplication of loaves. Our own participation—by way of the Holy Eucharist, God's gift to man—is the greatest privilege possible.

THREE

God's Greatest Gift

St. Augustine, the great saint who lived in the fourth century and was converted from his worldly ways through the unceasing prayers of his mother, St. Monica, once launched a spiritual teaching with what today's advertising moguls would call a "teaser." He said, "There is only one thing God does not know. He does not know how he could give us a gift greater than himself—and he has given us the gift of himself as bread in the Holy Eucharist."

We know that God is *omniscient*; he knows everything. Yet, it seems that in giving us the ultimate gift of himself in the Eucharist, God has exhausted his divine ingenuity. The gift of himself is not merely a spiritual gift, or *charism*. It is not even simply offering himself as a friend to us. Rather, God gives himself to us in the closest kind of intimacy—physically and spiritually—in the union called Communion.

Communion involves a physical, spiritual, and emotional intimacy in which God, who the heavens cannot contain, is totally contained within our heart and our body. This is a supernal marvel that only God could design. It is as if God's limitless love has, as it were, exhausted his own divine ingenuity in designing a way to get eminently close to his beloved human creatures, whom he has fashioned in his own image and likeness.

How little we appreciate this marvelous plan of God. How seldom we are thankful for it. How rarely we avail ourselves of God's gift to us, not only in terms of frequency but also in terms of fervor.

Psalm 78:25 speaks about "the bread of angels," referring to the life-sustaining manna in the wilderness. The Eucharist has been described as "the bread of angels that angels cannot receive." Our guardian angels look upon us as we receive Communion and experience a holy envy of us. Imagine, then, the great consternation of the guardian angel of a person who approaches the altar to receive Communion in a routine and devotionless way, who is concerned only with hurrying home to watch TV or read the paper. The angel might ask, "How could this person be so apathetic about receiving the God whom the universe cannot contain? How can this person be so oblivious and unresponsive to the tremendous power to change their lives—and even their health—through God's healing power? If I were receiving Communion, how differently I would react."

This thought-provoking insight should entice us to yearn for the Bread of God with the same fervor of Jesus' newly attracted disciples: When the divine "Loaf Keeper" told them of a bread far superior to the loaves miraculously multiplied to feed the multitude, their response was, "Lord, give us this bread always" (Jn 6:34, RSV). What fervor! This should be our heartfelt prayer also, today and every day. If we could see what happens in the spiritual realm when we receive Communion, if our faith were that strong (and no one's faith really is), we would be catapulted into ecstasy at Communion. We would be totally unaware of anything around us and be immersed in an experience akin to heaven itself!

This classic Augustinian insight—that God does not know how to give us a gift greater than himself—should alert us to the fact that this greatest gift is accompanied by incredible power. When the supreme gift is fully embraced by a human heart bursting with love, this power is available to us.

The Devotion of the Saints

The lives of the saints abound with examples of their love and devotion for the Eucharist. Indeed, their holiness, which enabled them to perceive this life through God's eyes, placed them in a unique position to recognize and respond to the priceless treasure—intimate union with God—available to them in the Eucharist.

This tradition of love and devotion began with the early Fathers of the Church. In the fourth century, St. John Chrysostom, a gifted preacher and patriarch of Constantinople, clearly grasped the profound meaning of the Eucharist, as evidenced by the words in one of his sermons: "To that Lord on whom the angels even dare not fix their eyes, to him we unite ourselves and we are made one body and one flesh."

St. Cyril of Alexandria, the champion of the doctrine of Mary's divine maternity and the mystery of the Incarnation at the Council of Ephesus in the fifth century, also elucidated the meaning of this mystery when he noted that "as two pieces of melted wax unite together, so a soul that receives Communion is so thoroughly united to Jesus that Jesus remains in it, and it in Jesus."

Later in history, St. Thomas Aquinas, the famous Dominican theologian of the thirteenth century whose treatises have left their imprint on theology to this day, described the Eucharist as "a sacrament of love and a token of the greatest love that God could give us."

St. Teresa of Avila was a Carmelite nun in the sixteenth century who led a major reform among the Carmelites of her day and who founded many monasteries throughout Spain. Because of her extensive writings on spiritual and mystical subjects, she was proclaimed a "Doctor of the Church" in 1970—the first woman to be honored by the Church with this title.

Regarding her devotion to the Eucharist, St. Teresa wrote that she could never doubt God's presence in the Eucharist, and that she chuckled to herself when she heard people saying they wished they had been around when Jesus was walking on the earth. "I know that I possess you in the Blessed Sacrament as truly as people did then, and I wonder what more anyone could possibly want."

St. Teresa also marveled at God's foresight in coming to us under the appearance of bread and wine: "How could I, a poor sinner who has offended you so often, dare to approach you, O Lord, if I beheld you in all your majesty? Under the appearance of bread, however, it is easy to approach you.... If you were not hidden, O Lord, who would dare approach you with such coldness, so unworthily, and with so many imperfections?"

St. Alphonsus Liguori, the founder of the Redemptorist order of priests in the eighteenth century, attributed his conversion at the age of twenty-six to his devotion to the Blessed Sacrament, which, he confessed, he practiced "with so much tepidity and in so imperfect a manner." He wrote one of his works, *Visits to the Blessed Sacrament*, out of gratitude for God's mercy toward him. He expressed his gratitude in these words: "Our most loving Redeemer, on the last night of his life, knowing that the long awaited time had arrived on which he should die for the love of man, had not the heart to leave us alone in this valley of tears. But in order that he might not be separated from us even by death, he would leave us his whole self as food in the Sacrament of the Altar, giving us to understand by this that, having given us this gift of infinite worth, he could give us nothing further to prove to us his love."

For many saints, this great love for the Eucharist took on almost superhuman dimensions. St. Gemma Galgani, a holy stigmatist who lived at the end of the nineteenth century, experienced a physical hunger for her daily Communion that was almost painful. If her Communion was postponed by even fifteen minutes, she felt as if she were going to faint from the intense hunger. It was a miraculous phenomenon by which her spiritual hunger was manifested in a physical way. On one occasion she exclaimed that if it were necessary to walk barefoot over hot coals all the way to church to receive Communion, she would do it gladly, rather than miss one day receiving her beloved Jesus in Holy Communion.

Similarly, at one point in her life, St. Teresa of Avila was plagued by a severe illness which occurred regularly every morning and evening. As a result of this illness, she was unable to hold down any food. Therefore, she was unable to receive Holy Communion at morning Mass. This was a source of great anguish for St. Teresa, since her desire for the Eucharist was so great that she used to say that neither fire nor sword could deter her from receiving her divine Lord. She pleaded with the Lord to heal her, knowing that his desire to come into her heart was even greater than her desire to receive him in Holy Communion. Jesus healed her to the extent that she did not experience the illness in the morning; she was able to receive our Lord in Holy Communion at that time. However, she continued to have attacks in the evening. St. Teresa felt that the evening attacks were a sign by which God was clearly indicating to her the purpose for which he had healed her.

St. Philip Neri was an Italian priest whose apostolate in Rome in the sixteenth century was characterized by a contagious joy. He spent many hours in ecstasy before the Blessed Sacrament. He experienced such an intense desire to receive the Eucharist at morning Mass that he often was unable to sleep at night because of his anticipation of receiving Jesus the next morning. Moreover, he used to drink from the chalice with such great love that he had a hard time tearing himself away from it. Consequently, he gradually wore off the gilding on the rim of the chalice and even left the imprint of his teeth there.

St. John Berchmans was a young Belgian Jesuit who died at the age of twenty-two in 1621, and was canonized in 1888. He too was noted for his exuberant joy, and is honored today as the patron saint of Mass servers and one of the patron saints of youth. One of his biographers reported that St. John

Berchmans, after a few days without taking the sacrament, felt a "hunger that could not be satiated except by Communion."

It is hard to find many souls today whose love even remotely approaches such an intensity. It is not surprising that St. Alphonsus says, "One Holy Communion is enough to make you a saint if you receive it with all the love of which you are capable." Some saints were given special graces to experience a mystical love in its deeper dimensions, causing them to exclaim, "Stop, God, stop this love. It's killing me. I'm going to die." Often they would experience one of the four types of ecstasy called a *fugue*, a state in which they felt as if their souls were being pulled right out of their bodies by the magnetism of God's love. This mystical experience was so deep they felt as if they were about to die from love.

It is possible that, if we used our full capacity for love when receiving Communion, it would indeed kill us. We receive Communion hundreds, maybe thousands, of times in our lifetime, and still we are not saints because, at best, we use only the tiniest fraction of our capacity for love.

St. Anthony Claret, the founder of the Claretian Congregation, to which I belong, was a great saint. He wrote 144 books, preached twenty-five thousand sermons, and was confessor to Queen Isabella II of Spain. He was archbishop of Santiago, Cuba, and he predicted the advent of communism. He worked many miracles and accomplished more work than any twenty persons could be expected to accomplish in a lifetime. He spent many hours before the tabernacle in prayer late into the night, in preparation for his Mass and for his reception of Communion the following morning.

Because of his remarkable love for the Eucharist, for the last nine years of his life St. Anthony was given the mystical privilege of miraculously retaining the sacred host in his breast, uncorrupted and undissolved, from one Communion to the next, in honor of the nine months Mary had Jesus within her during her pregnancy. He was a walking tabernacle, a fact that his spiritual director revealed only after St. Anthony's death. When St. Anthony Claret attended the First Vatican Council in 1870 as an archbishop, a bishop from Canada miraculously perceived the real presence of Christ in him and felt compelled to genuflect before him—not to adore St. Anthony Claret, but to adore the eucharistic presence of Christ within him. The power of this eucharistic presence within him was manifest in many ways and on many occasions.

When people have an extraordinary devotion to the Eucharist, God does some extraordinary things in their lives. Although they may never be in the spotlight of admiration from those around them, they lead lives of hidden sanctity, and they exert a powerful spiritual influence on others. The sanctifying power that God releases in them does not stay within them; it moves out and spreads to others. The lives of many saints testify to this.

Back in the twelfth century a heresy known as Albigensianism had made significant inroads in parts of Europe. Among other things, its adherents denied the real presence of Christ in the Eucharist. St. Anthony of Padua (who was so renowned as a great preacher that his tongue is still preserved incorrupt in Padua, Italy) was once preaching in a town square. A heckler named Bovillo suddenly confronted him and screamed out, "I'll believe in your doctrine of Christ's real presence in the host if, after starving my donkey for three days, he kneels before your Blessed Sacrament and ignores the hay I'll put next to him!"

St. Anthony took him up on that challenge. The man starved his donkey for three days. In the meantime, St. Anthony fasted and prayed. At the agreed upon time, Bovillo brought his starving donkey to the town square to face the pile of fresh hay, with the Blessed Sacrament next to it. All the townspeople turned out to see what would happen. Bovillo prodded his donkey to eat the hay, while St. Anthony spoke softly to the donkey, commanding him to adore Jesus in the Blessed Sacrament. To the great astonishment of all present, the donkey fell to his knees before the Blessed Sacrament. Bovillo kept prodding his donkey to eat the hay by holding it close to his mouth, but the donkey refused. At that point Bovillo, shaken and pale, fell to his knees in devout belief.

A few years ago someone recounted a much more recent story that made a deep impression on me. When the Communists came to power in North Vietnam, a group of Communist soldiers barged into a cloistered convent of nuns. Their intention was to evict the nuns and convert the cloister into barracks. The mother superior confronted the intruding soldiers and demanded that they respect the cloister.

"Please leave us alone," she pleaded. "We have the King of Kings living with us in our chapel. Jesus is alive here, and we don't want to surrender this building to you because of that." The sergeant in the group said scornfully, "Where is this King of Kings, this Jesus, you talk about?"

The mother superior took him to the chapel and pointed to

the tabernacle: "He's in that tabernacle, reserved in the Blessed Sacrament." The sergeant picked up a rifle, aimed it, and shot directly into the tabernacle. The echo of that shot had not died down before that sergeant was dead of a heart attack right there in the chapel.

Miracles of the Eucharist

History is replete with events that bespeak the power of the Eucharist to change the lives of those who believe and love, and also to change the lives of many who do not believe or love. There are numerous miracles that God has performed through the centuries to demonstrate to us his real presence in the Eucharist. Many of these miracles have been written up in the annals of history. Some were only momentary and have fallen into obscurity because they served their purpose at the time. Others, however, continue to this day, still serving as a testimony of God's real presence in the Eucharist.I would like to recount two of these outstanding miracles that have withstood the test of time.

At the beginning of the eighth century, a priest was celebrating Mass at a monastery in Lanciano, Italy. Although he was reputed to be an intelligent and well-educated man, for some time he had been entertaining serious doubts regarding the real presence of Jesus in the Eucharist. When he spoke the words of Consecration at Mass on that particular day, he realized that the host was suddenly changed into a circle of flesh and that the wine in the chalice was transformed into blood. Weeping joyously, he invited those present to approach the altar to witness this miracle, and word quickly spread about this revelation.

The host and the blood have been carefully preserved over the centuries at the Church of the Miracle in Lanciano, and the church has been the site of pilgrimages ever since. Many studies of this miracle have been conducted, including one in 1970. This particular study was performed according to the strict guidelines that govern modern scientific research.

Scientists learned at that time that, even though the lunette containing the flesh was not hermetically sealed, the flesh was still intact and was identified as human muscular tissue from the heart wall, without any trace of any preservation agent. The blood type was AB. These scientists were amazed at the expert, tangential cut of the heart tissue —a cut that could only be made by someone who is intimately acquainted with human anatomy and who has extensive experience in dissection.

When they examined the blood, they noted it had not suffered from any spoilage, even though it was also kept over the centuries in a container not hermetically sealed. Normally blood is quickly altered through spoilage and decay. The blood was also found to be of human origin, and the same blood type as the flesh—AB.

Today, pilgrims to the Church of the Miracle in Lanciano can climb a staircase at the back of the altar to view the tabernacle and gaze upon the miraculous Eucharist in the reliquary. This miracle has continued for almost thirteen hundred years.

In another example of miraculous manifestation, seven hundred years ago a woman in Portugal learned that her husband was being unfaithful to her. She sought the advice of a fortune teller for dealing with the situation. The fortune teller told the woman she could help her if she would only deliver into her hands a consecrated host. The woman went to the local church, received Communion, removed the host from her mouth, and hid it in her veil. She fully intended to give it to the fortune teller. However, the host began to bleed profusely. People near her noticed the blood dripping around her and, believing she was ill, hastened to help her. The woman was so frightened that she quickly ran home where she hid the bloody veil with the host in a trunk.

That evening, a mysterious light began to emanate from the trunk. When the woman saw the light, she confessed her sin to her husband. Together, they knelt in adoration until morning, when they called in their parish priest. News about the miracle spread among the people, and the host was reverently taken to the church in a procession. There it was placed in a tabernacle until the parish priest could determine what he should do with it. When the tabernacle was opened a few days later, the host was found to be miraculously enclosed in a crystal lunette.

The whole episode was carefully scrutinized by church authorities, who saw no reason to doubt the supernatural nature of what had occurred. Eventually the host was placed in a special monstrance, where it has been preserved for over seven hundred years at what is now known as the Church of the Holy Miracle in Santarem, Portugal. Amazingly, the host continues to bleed at times. It is irregularly shaped, with small veins running from top to bottom. People who have observed and studied this phenomenon report that the blood that collects at the bottom of the crystal lunette in the monstrance sometimes has the color of fresh blood, and at other times has the color of dried blood. I personally have had the privilege of giving a group of pilgrims benediction with this host.

The phenomenon of bleeding hosts (often reminding us of the bleeding heart of Christ, anguishing over the sin of mankind) is one that is occurring in many places in our time. Two occurrences are especially noteworthy. Even though the phenomena occurring at these places are still being studied by Church authorities and no official pronouncement has been made as to their veracity, they have occurred spontaneously in the presence of many reliable witnesses, thereby discounting the possibility of any fraud. In fact, they have been a source of consolation for many believers, and a source of conversion for many nonbelievers. They testify to the fact that the Lord continues to work in amazing ways among us today.

The first case involves a young girl, Audrey Santo of Worcester, Massachusetts, who was born in 1983. Audrey was the victim of a tragic near-drowning accident when she was three years old. She now lives confined to her bed in a coma-like state, and receives care around the clock from her family and a staff of nurses. Though unable to speak or move, this silent, suffering child has been used by God in a special way over the years. Many alleged miracles and mystical experiences have surrounded her, and many healings have been reported among the thousands of people who have visited her. At least three of Audrey's nurses have become Catholic after caring for her. Countless priests, theologians, skeptics, and ordinary laypeople have been touched by God through this little girl.

However, I would like to draw particular attention to just

one aspect of Audrey's story. For most of her life, Audrey has been lying in bed before the Blessed Sacrament, reserved in her room by special permission of the local bishop. Moreover, she has received Holy Communion every day since she was five years old, her only solid food since that time. The Eucharist has clearly been a focal point for most of her life.

On four different occasions since 1994, consecrated hosts in her room have mysteriously changed in appearance and have begun to bleed. On the first occasion, a scientific expert from a research laboratory was called in to investigate this event. The expert found a one-inch size host inside a glass reliquary in the tabernacle with an irregular brownish stain on half of it, similar to dried blood. However, he noticed a smear of what looked like fresh bright-red blood on the inside surface of the glass reliquary. Careful not to touch the consecrated host itself, the expert decided to examine the smear on the glass under his microscope. The red spot appeared as coagulated blood under the microscope, with red cells attached tightly to each other. Five people witnessed all stages of the investigation, and the whole process was recorded on videotape.

On another occasion, a priest who is the main spiritual director for the Santo family was concelebrating Mass at the Santo home with two visiting priests, and with several other priests and laypeople present. At the moment of the consecration, as he elevated the large host, the priest noticed that a smaller host on the paten had changed color. Upon closer examination, he realized that there was blood in the center of the small host. The three priests were overwhelmed, and one began to cry. Those in attendance at that Mass were shocked, since it seemed rather clear to them that a eucharistic miracle was apparently taking place.

Out of respect to Church authorities, the Santo family wishes that these phenomena of bleeding hosts not be called "eucharistic miracles," since they believe Church authorities are the only ones competent to make such a judgment. Naturally, it has been hard to deny this reality to the many faithful who have visited the Santo home, including many priests and theologians.

The second case worthy of highlighting involves Julia Kim, a devout Catholic mother of four children who lives in Naju, Korea. Mrs. Kim maintains that she has been visited many times since 1985 by both Jesus and Mary, and has received messages from them to share with the public at large. Church authorities and theologians who have examined these messages have found no fault with them. The messages are essentially calls to repentance, including fervent pleas for people to receive the Eucharist devoutly. The messages have often mentioned that people are receiving Communion either indifferently or sacrilegiously because of a lack of understanding or outright disbelief in Jesus' real presence in the Eucharist.

Many apparent miracles have occurred in Naju over the years, and they all lend support to Mrs. Kim's claims. For example, a statue of Our Lady that is owned by the Kim family shed tears of blood for seven hundred days. Samples of these tears of blood were tested in the medical laboratory of Seoul National University and were found to be human blood. In her messages to Mrs. Kim, Mary has said that she is weeping constantly because of our failure to love God and to love each other; because of the numerous innocent unborn babies being killed in their mothers' wombs; and because of the many souls who refuse to repent.

When the statue ceased to shed tears of blood, a fragrant oil started to flow from the head of the statue. This phenomenon also continued for seven hundred days. Mary told Mrs. Kim that this fragrance represents her presence among us, and her love and friendship for us.

When Mrs. Kim first saw a vision of Jesus suffering and bleeding profusely on the cross for the redemption of sinners, she was so moved by love that she asked the Lord to allow her a life of suffering. Since then, she frequently has suffered excruciating pain. At one point, she received the stigmata while praying before a crucifix. Later she prayed that the wounds would become invisible because of the attention they attracted. Her prayer was granted and, purportedly, she continues to suffer from these invisible wounds.

In addition to these apparently supernatural phenomena, other phenomena have occurred involving the Eucharist. These phenomena merit special attention, especially in light of the eucharistic nature of the many messages Mrs. Kim has shared. On numerous occasions since 1988, the sacred host that Mrs. Kim received during Mass turned into visible flesh and began bleeding in her mouth. This phenomenon, witnessed by hundreds of people, has been photographed and videotaped as well. It was reported that the Holy Father himself witnessed this phenomenon during a Mass that he celebrated in the Vatican on October 31, 1995, at which Mrs. Kim was present.

Another witness is the Most Reverend Roman Danylak, a bishop who was the apostolic administrator for the eparchy of

Toronto for Ukrainian Catholics at the time. Bishop Danylak has issued an official statement regarding what he saw at the Mass that he concelebrated in Naju, Korea, on September 22, 1995, with Fr. Aloysius Chang from Korea and Fr. Joseph Finn, a retired priest from the Diocese of London, Ontario, Canada:

As we continued to distribute Holy Communion to the others present, we heard the sudden sobbing of one of the women assisting at Mass. The sacred host received by Julia Kim was changed to living flesh and blood. Fr. Joseph Finn, who had remained at the altar during the Communion of the faithful, was observing Julia; he noted that at the moment he turned to observe Julia, he saw the white edge of the host disappearing, and changing into the substance of living flesh.

Fr. Chang and I returned to Julia. The host had changed to dark, red, living flesh, and blood was flowing from it. After Mass, Julia shared with us that she experienced the Divine Flesh as a thick consistency and a copious flowing of blood, more so than on the occasion of previous miracles of the changing of the host into bleeding flesh. We remained in silence and prayer; all present had the opportunity of viewing and venerating the miraculous host. After some moments, I asked Julia to swallow and consume the host. And after the Mass, Julia explained that the host had become large and fleshy, and that she consumed it with difficulty. The taste of blood remained in her mouth for some time. I then asked that she be given a glass of water from the miraculous source of water nearby. As she drank the water, her finger touched her lips, and a trace of blood was visible on her finger. She rinsed her finger in the water and drank it.

Bishop Danylak later reported that the woman who cried out during the Mass was miraculously healed from intense back and shoulder pains at that time.

The phenomenon of bleeding hosts is not the only eucharistic miracle to occur in Naju. On November 24, 1994, the Most Reverend Giovanni Bulaitis, an archbishop who is the Apostolic Pro-Nuncio to Korea, visited Naju in his capacity as the official representative of the Holy Father. In the presence of the archbishop, seven priests, and about seventy laypeople who were praying in the chapel, the Blessed Mother appeared to Mrs. Kim, gave her some messages, and instructed her to ask the archbishop and her spiritual director (who was also present) for their blessing.

Then the Blessed Mother had St. Michael the Archangel bring the Holy Eucharist to the Apostolic Pro-Nuncio through Mrs. Kim. The angel was visible only to Mrs. Kim, but everyone was able to see the Holy Eucharist suddenly appearing between Mrs. Kim's fingers. The host was a large one, like those the priests use during Mass, and was already broken in two when it was given to her. The host was broken into smaller pieces by the archbishop so that everyone in the chapel could receive Holy Communion. Some of those present later testified to their total amazement and awe, and said that it was an experience that defied human description. A piece of the host was placed in a pyx for preservation.

As Mrs. Kim was returning to her home to write down the messages she had received, the Blessed Mother summoned her back to the chapel and asked her to receive the Holy Eucharist a second time, while holding the hands of the archbishop and her spiritual director. This time she received a smaller host that appeared out of nowhere, standing upright on her tongue. The archbishop picked up the host and showed it to the people present. Photos were taken, and the host was placed in a pyx for preservation. The archbishop later said that he was so overwhelmed with joy and hope that he could not sleep for three nights in a row!

Almost a year later, on June 30, 1995, thousands of pilgrims converged on Naju to celebrate the tenth anniversary of the weeping statue. An overnight prayer meeting was organized in the chapel. At about 3:45 A.M., Mrs. Kim stood up and stretched out her hands, as if trying to grab something. Some present in the chapel saw sparks of light come from the crucifix at that moment, and others heard a noise like a brief hailstorm. Everyone saw seven hosts coming down, which bypassed Mrs. Kim's hands and landed on the altar in front of a statue of Our Lady. Mrs. Kim later testified that, while praying, she saw the wooden image of Jesus on the cross turning into the live Jesus, with bleeding occurring at seven places on his body: his two hands, his two feet, his side, his forehead, and his heart. Soon the blood at the seven wounds turned into white, round hosts and descended onto the altar.

When the local archbishop was informed of this latest occurrence, he instructed Mrs. Kim and some others to consume the seven hosts. Two days later, Mrs. Kim and six others received Communion. When Mrs. Kim received Communion, the host began to bleed.

A couple of years later, on June 12, 1997, Bishop Paul Chang Yeol Kim of Cheju, Korea, was visiting the chapel and was praying with several other people in front of the Blessed Mother's statue. Suddenly, a large host descended from above. In total amazement and joy, Bishop Kim worshiped and prayed before the Eucharist, and later blessed with the Eucharist those who were present. The Eucharist was placed in a monstrance so that people could worship it. Later it was moved to the local archdiocesan office.

On the Eucharist was an image of the Sacred Heart of Jesus encircled by thorns. Two drops of blood were flowing from the wounds on the heart. A small cross was located above the heart, and a flame of fire under the cross, representing Jesus' love for us. Bishop Kim visited the local archbishop and reported the details of this miracle to him.

Hundreds of stories like these have been authenticated historically and scientifically. Through them God shows us the reality of his presence in the Eucharist. Like doubting St. Thomas, some people have to witness miracles before they will believe. Even Jesus himself noted, "Unless you people see signs and wonders, you will not believe" (Jn 4:48). They refuse to believe in faith; they want scientific proof. Yet, as Jesus said to St. Thomas, "Blessed are those who have not seen and yet have believed" (Jn 20:29).

Let us cultivate humble and faith-filled love for Jesus, with consummate gratitude for this greatest of many gifts to us. The very word Eucharist means *good gift* in early Greek; in later Greek it connoted *thanksgiving for a good gift* (see Jn 6:23). Let our hearts surge with gratitude to a God who gives us nothing less than his very self!

Four Ways to Stymie Grace

In 1 Thessalonians 5:19 St. Paul reminds us, "Do not quench the Spirit." Jesus does not want his spirit to be quenched but to spread: "I have come to set the earth on fire, and how I wish it were already blazing" (Lk 12:49). Jesus wants this spiritual energy—this fire of love—to be activated and enkindled in us. Unfortunately, we can quench this spark of grace before it produces the effect God intends.

This is particularly true when we receive Jesus in the Eucharist. Before explaining how we can fully experience the awesome power of grace in this sacrament, it may be helpful to examine the ways we inhibit the release of God's power in our lives. Needless to say, because of our sinful nature, we often unwittingly erect barriers to God's working in us and through us. He wants to cast his fire of love over the earth, but we often provide only fuel dampened with worldliness and sin.

There are four principal ways in which we can stymie the flow of grace that is available to us in the Eucharist.

Limited Devotion to the Eucharist

First, we can limit God's grace from working in us by receiving Communion with limited fervor, devotion, or love. It is so easy for apathy, lethargy, or routine to characterize our sacramental life. Yet, Holy Communion should be for us a fire that enkindles love, devotion, and spiritual joy in our hearts.

Jesus tells us to *hunger* after the bread he gives us (Jn 6:27), which is his very flesh for the life of the world (v. 51). Hunger implies a yearning, and there certainly is nothing apathetic about that! Indeed, a person who is really starving cannot think about anything except food. We should have this same yearning within us, but unfortunately this longing is frequently missing when we receive Communion. As a result, our reception of the Eucharist often ends up being hardly more than a religious exercise that we perform dutifully rather than devotionally.

Essentially, it is a question of quality. We inhibit the action of God's grace in us because the quality of our fervor, devotion, or love is simply not up to par. But this was not always the case. In the early Church there was tremendous fervor because there was tremendous faith. In Acts 2:42, St. Luke tells us that the early Christians "*devoted* themselves to the teaching of the apostles and to the communal life, to the breaking of the bread and the prayers" (NAB, emphasis added). The word "devoted" implies a fervent faith! Galatians 5:6 (NAB) tells us what matters is "faith working through love." As we have already seen, *love* of the Eucharist is based on *faith* in the Eucharist. Today our faith is extremely weak. Even today's strongest Christians, who think they have great faith, have much less faith than that which prevailed in the early Church when miracles were happening continually. Because people in the early Church expected miracles at Mass on Sunday, they saw miracles when they attended Mass—especially healing miracles.

For the first eight centuries in the history of the Church, faith was at a high pitch. Charisms were routinely being manifested, especially in the post-Communion period of the Mass. St. Augustine, who lived in the fourth century, witnessed these charisms, or extraordinary powers, such as healing, given to Christians by the Holy Spirit for the good of the Church. In fact, during one Mass he saw seventy-three people cured instantly of serious illnesses. He knew then and there that the charisms were not just meant for the apostolic times of the first century.

As a result, St. Augustine changed his theology to correspond more directly to sacred Scripture. He realized that, just as healing had been an integral part of Jesus' ministry, healing should also be a part of his own ministry. He also realized that Jesus' power could exert its effect on everyone who touched him.

In Luke 8:43-48, we read about a woman who had been hemorrhaging for twelve years. She went from doctor to doctor seeking a cure, spending all her money to no avail. No one could heal her (v. 43). One day, when Jesus was besieged by a crowd, this woman managed to get close enough to Jesus to touch his cloak. Immediately, her bleeding stopped. Jesus turned and asked, "Who touched me? Someone has touched me; for I know that power has gone out from me" (v. 46). Fearfully and sheepishly, the woman stepped forward and admitted she was the one who had touched Jesus. She explained to the crowd why she had touched him in order to be healed. And she was. Jesus told her, "Daughter, your faith has saved you; go in peace."

St. Augustine knew that Jesus' healing power was available to anyone who, like this woman, reached out with the requisite faith and touched Jesus, especially in the sacrament of the Eucharist.

This expectant faith is not that predominant today, when people rather routinely shuffle into church, attend Mass, and receive Communion before dashing home to read the news-paper and watch television. By going through these "churchy" motions, they feel they have paid their debt to God. Pope Paul VI succinctly summarized this attitude when he said, "Unfortunately, today many engage in the liturgical service not as a beautiful ritual, but as pharisaic ritualism." Many people go automatically through the external motions with very little internal fervor. Their participation is often apathetic and lethar-gic. They do not have the incandescent "faith working through love" (Gal 5:6, NAB) that they should have when they engage in the Liturgy of the Eucharist, and especially when they receive Communion. They might be touching Jesus in the sacrament of the Eucharist, but they are not being healed. They might pray, "Heal me, heal members of my family, and heal my mar-riage," but they are not exerting any real faith that could educe such healing. Their faith is merely a faith of urgency, not a faith of loving expectancy. Sadly, they are far from experiencing that faith which would enable them to tap into the full power of the sacrament.

Why is this the case? In January 1992, the Gallup organization conducted a scientific poll among 519 Catholics to assess what Catholics in the United States believe about Holy Communion. The poll had a margin of error of plus or minus five percentage points. Alarmingly, the poll showed that most Catholics were seriously confused about one of the most fundamental beliefs of the Catholic Church. When asked to choose among four different options the one that best described their belief regarding the Eucharist, only 30 percent of those surveyed chose the traditional Catholic teaching, namely, that they were receiving the Body and Blood of Jesus Christ under the appearance of bread and wine (by a *substance* change called transubstantiation). Another 29 percent felt they were receiving bread and wine which merely symbolize the spirit and teachings of Jesus, and in doing so, were expressing their attachment to his person and his works. Ten percent thought that, in receiving Holy Communion, they were receiving bread and wine in which Jesus is really and truly present—the traditional Lutheran understanding of the Eucharist (impanation or consubstantiation). Finally, 24 percent believed they were receiving what has become the Body and Blood of Christ *because of* their personal belief, which reflects the traditional Calvinist doctrine.

Two years later, in April 1994, a New York Times/CBS News poll queried a sample of American Catholics and asked them, "Which of the following comes closest to what you believe takes place at Mass: (1) the bread and wine are changed into the Body and Blood of Christ, or (2) the bread and wine are symbolic reminders of Christ?" The results of this poll were equally dismal and confirmed the results of the earlier poll. Only 34 percent believed that the bread and wine were changed into Christ's Body and Blood. Another 63 percent said that they believed that the bread and wine were symbolic reminders of Christ.

Regardless of which poll you look at, about two out of every three Catholics do not believe in the real, physical, eucharistic presence. Two out of every three Catholics do not believe Jesus' words, "The bread that I will give is my flesh for the life of the world.... Unless you eat the flesh of the Son of Man and drink his blood, you do not have life within you. Whoever eats my flesh and drinks my blood has eternal life, and I will raise him on the last day. For my flesh is true food, and my blood is true drink" (Jn 6:51, 53-55, NAB). These people would probably be somewhat surprised to learn that they fit the classic description of a heretic as defined by Canon 751 of the canon law of the Catholic Church! If two out of every three Catholics do not believe these words of Jesus, how are they going to have any true devotion? And how can they experience the *healing power* of the Eucharist? These people lack a basic level of faith, and a basic belief in God's revealed truth is missing from their lives.

The real presence of Jesus Christ in the Holy Eucharist is a great mystery, and we should strive to cultivate our faith in this mystery, which is a basic doctrine of our Catholic faith. Scripture makes numerous references to the fact that Jesus is truly, really, and substantially present in the Eucharist under the outward appearances of bread and wine. As we have already seen, the sixth chapter of the Gospel of John is Jesus' most explicit and unambiguous teaching on his real presence in the Eucharist. The other Gospel writers all echo John's account of Jesus' teaching. When recounting the events at the Last Supper, they all unequivocally affirm that Jesus' words were, "This *is* my body..." and "This *is* my blood..." (emphasis added).

Likewise, St. Paul also makes several references to belief in the real presence of Jesus in the Eucharist in the tenth and eleventh chapters of his First Letter to the Corinthians. In 1 Corinthians 10:16, (NAB) he writes: "The cup of blessing that we bless, is it not a participation in the blood of Christ? The bread that we break, is it not a participation in the body of Christ?" Later, in 1 Corinthians 11:27-29, (NAB) he admonishes the Christians of Corinth with these words: "Therefore, whoever eats the bread or drinks the cup of the Lord unworthily will have to answer for the body and blood of the Lord. A person should examine himself, and so eat the bread and drink the cup. For anyone who eats and drinks without discerning the body, eats and drinks judgment on himself."

Clearly, Jesus does not speak about a symbolic presence or merely a memorial presence in Scripture, but a real, physical presence. St. Gregory Nazianzen, a great theologian who lived in the fourth century, once wrote that the Eucharist "is the food that hungers to be eaten." It is only fitting that reciprocally we should hunger after that food. Without truly believing in the real presence of Jesus in the Eucharist, how can anyone hunger or earnestly seek after the bread from heaven? Without faith in Jesus' presence in the Eucharist, how can there be any faith in his healing power in the Eucharist? And without any measure of fervor or devotion, how can anyone expect any kind of healing? Regrettably, many people do not even think of healing as available through the Eucharist, or know how Communion can be a source of healing for them. A tremendous amount of potential energy is never actualized in the sacrament of the Eucharist. It lies dormant, like all the drops of water in the ocean that harbor prodigious quantities of energy but await the day when scientists discover ways of releasing and directing the tremendous force they store. Few people may realize that a cup of water would suffice to produce enough energy to equal that of a nuclear bomb. Likewise, few people realize that through the sacrament of the Eucharist we have access to enormous spiritual power. Many people are not tapping into that spiritual power because of an apathy based upon a lack of faith.

Scripture describes the end times in various places, and Jesus referred to some of the signs that will characterize the end times. Some of these signs, unfortunately, can be observed today. One sign is a lack of faith. In Luke 18:8 (NAB) Jesus asks, "But when the Son of Man comes, will he find faith on earth?" Elsewhere Jesus tells us that a lack of love will be another sign of the end times. In Matthew 24:12 he warns us that "because of the increase of evildoing, the love of many will grow cold." In Galatians 5:6 (NAB), St. Paul tells us, "For in Christ Jesus neither circumcision nor uncircumcision counts for anything, but only faith working through love." The Greek expression for "faith working through love" (Gal 5:6) can also be rendered as *"faith energized by love."*

If there is neither much faith nor much love, how can much power be released? How can potential power be released as actual power? The first obstacle to the release of grace in the sacrament of the Eucharist is receiving it with only limited love, that is, fervor or devotion.

Infrequent Reception of the Eucharist

The second way in which we stymie the grace available to us in the sacrament of the Eucharist is by receiving Communion infrequently. As we described, the first way in which we can stymie grace refers to quality; this second way refers to quantity—the number of times in a given period that a person receives Communion. Pope John Paul II has reminded us that in normal situations anyone who calls himself or herself a good Catholic should receive Communion at least once a week.

In John 6:57 Jesus says, "Just as the living Father sent me and I have life because of the Father, so also the one who feeds on me will have life because of me" (NAB). The word "feeds" implies an ongoing action, and this is precisely what Jesus meant. We need to feed our bodies at regular and frequent intervals in order to sustain life and enjoy full health. We cannot nourish our bodies at sporadic intervals without eventually suffering some deterioration in our physical condition. The same principle applies to our spiritual being. We cannot feed on the Bread of Life at infrequent intervals and flourish spiritually. On the contrary, we need to receive Jesus in the Eucharist frequently to sustain the flow of grace needed to nourish us spiritually and to transform the potential spiritual energy of the sacrament into actual spiritual energy.

Not Partaking of the Eucharist

The third way in which we stymie the action of grace is by simply not receiving Communion at all. In some cases, of course, it is physically impossible to receive Communion for some good reason. For example, a person might be hospitalized for an extended period of time and unable to receive Communion. Another example would be a person who is incarcerated in a prison where there is little or no opportunity to attend Mass or receive Communion. An even more common example would be the millions of people around the world who reside in mission territories that are not yet served by any priest.

Needless to say, God understands that these people do not have access to him in the Eucharist. Even though they cannot physically receive Communion, God attaches great importance to their loving desire, which, if present, would provide for them, exceptionally, a "spiritual communion." There are other cases too where people never receive Communion because of real ignorance. They simply lack the basic theological or spiritual knowledge needed to recognize the importance of regular reception of the Eucharist. But it is most frequently the case that people do not receive Communion because they simply are not interested in doing so. In these situations, God ultimately judges each person according to the degree of malice that is present in the situation. It is impossible to sin without malice, and there are different degrees of malice, as evidenced in this Scripture: "All wrongdoing is sin, but there is sin that is not deadly" (1 Jn 5:17, NAB).

Receiving the Eucharist Sacrilegiously

This leads us to the fourth way in which we can stymie the flow of grace: by receiving Communion sacrilegiously in a state of serious, unrepented, and unconfessed sin. Examples of serious sin abound: having an abortion, committing adultery, living in an invalid marriage, missing Mass on Sunday without good reason. Those who commit such serious sin, and fail to confess and repent of their sin before receiving Communion again are receiving the sacrament sacrilegiously. Such sacrilegious Communions can cause not just great spiritual damage to the soul but even physical damage to the body.

St. Paul reminds us of this in 1 Corinthians 11:27-30 (NAB): "Therefore whoever eats the bread or drinks the cup of the Lord unworthily will have to answer for the body and blood of the Lord. A person should examine himself, and so eat the bread and drink the cup. For anyone who eats and drinks without discerning the body, eats and drinks judgment on himself. That is why many among you are ill and infirm and a considerable number are dying."

The last sentence of the above quote from St. Paul is significant. St. Paul is speaking about the opposite of healing—the destruction of the body. Many people, he says, are weak, sick, or even dead because they received Communion unworthily or sacrilegiously. These words tell us how sacred Communion is. We are not simply eating a piece of "blessed bread." After the consecration, the bread is no longer bread; it is the Bread of Life, the Body of Christ, a person, not a thing. That is why St. Paul addresses the seriousness of receiving Communion unworthily when writing to the Christians of Corinth.

What does it mean to receive Communion in an unworthy manner? There are two kinds of unworthiness. In one sense, we are all unworthy to receive Communion because of our human nature. No human being, even the sinless Virgin Mary, could ever be worthy of receiving Communion in the strict sense of the word, because a person would have to be God to be worthy of receiving God. In this sense we are all unworthy.

The second sense in which we are unworthy to receive Communion is the unworthiness to which St. Paul refers. A person is unworthy to receive Communion when he or she is in a state of enmity with God by having committed a mortal sin but not repented of that sin. We read in 1 John 5:16b (NAB): "There is such a thing as deadly sin." The Latin word for death is *mors*, from which we get the word *mortal*, as in mortal sin. Not every sin is deadly; not every sin is a mortal sin. If you swipe a penny, you do not commit a mortal sin. If you rob a bank, you are committing a mortal sin. There is a great difference between the two.

There are different degrees of sin. But anything that is a serious violation of God's law, that a person commits with full knowledge and complete consent, is mortal sin. Obvious examples would be abortion or murder. Such sin creates enmity with God until repentance takes place. People who are at enmity with God, who are living in a state of mortal sin, are excluded from Christ's kingdom and destined to the eternal death of hell. The only way they can change their destiny is by making an act of repentance and receiving God's forgiveness.

St. Paul elaborates on this unworthiness to receive

Communion when he tells us in 1 Corinthians 10:21 (NAB), "You cannot drink the cup of the Lord and also the cup of demons. You cannot partake of the table of the Lord and of the table of demons." People who are involved in occultism or witchcraft have clearly aligned themselves with demonic forces. But we know that people who are in serious sin have also aligned themselves with the devil because St. John writes, "Whoever sins belongs to the devil, because the devil has sinned from the beginning" (1 Jn 3:8, NAB). As we have already observed, St. Paul tells us that these people cannot eat at the table of the Lord because they are unworthy to do so, and they face some serious consequences, including possibly even an early death, if they do (see 1 Corinthians 11:30).

When people knowingly refuse to believe in the real presence of the Eucharist, they fall into the type of unworthiness to which St. Paul refers. As we have already noted in unequivocal terms, these people are guilty of heresy according to the definition contained in Canon 751 of the canon law of the Catholic Church. Such thinking is contrary to God's teaching in the Bible, as well as the unremitting teaching of the Catholic Church from the time of Christ. For twenty centuries the Church has taught nothing but the real presence. Tragically, nonacceptance of this doctrine poisons two-thirds of the Catholic population in the United States.

It is interesting to note that, in the course of the history of eucharistic theology, there have been 152 different interpretations of those four words, "This is my body," and that ninety of those interpretations are currently being used by various Christian religions today. Yet the teaching of the Catholic

Church has never wavered throughout the centuries. The Catholic Church has always taken those words literally, which are supported by all the other scriptural cross-references to the doctrine of the Holy Eucharist. Catholics are truly "fundamentalists" when it comes to the Eucharist—more so than almost all Protestant fundamentalists on this issue! This theology is the basis for our devotion to the Eucharist.

In summary, these are the four ways in which we can fail to cooperate with grace when receiving the sacrament of the Eucharist: First, we can let a certain apathy set in by receiving Communion with limited fervor. Secondly, we can receive the Eucharist too infrequently. Thirdly, we can fail to receive the Holy Sacrament at all. Fourthly, we can receive it sacrilegiously.

By way of analogy, this great gift of God can be rendered ineffectual, to a greater or lesser degree, in four ways. First, fervorless reception of the Eucharist is like gasoline in a car that has a wastefully inefficient engine. We are not using the full capacity of the gasoline when the engine is not efficient. Secondly, infrequent reception is like gasoline in a car that is seldom used. The gasoline is there, but it is not being transformed into actual energy. In the third case, where the sacrament is totally neglected, the sacrament is like gasoline in an abandoned car in a junkyard. It is not being used at all. Finally, when the Eucharist is received sacrilegiously, it is tantamount to using gasoline to drive a car with a defective motor, which is further damaged by being driven. In these four ways we can truncate the flow of God's grace and show ourselves truly unthankful (and the word "Eucharist" means *thanksgiving*) for the presence of Jesus himself, God's "indescribable gift" (2 Cor 9:15).

FIVE

How to Receive the Eucharist Devoutly

A religion teacher once gave her fourth-grade students a rather unusual assignment. She asked them to write a paragraph describing how they would spend the day if Jesus came to visit them. The children put their heads down and began to write furiously. However, one boy began to wave his hand in the air. "What is it, Johnny?" the teacher asked. Johnny replied, "How do you spell 'Toys R Us?'"

What would we do if Jesus came to spend a day with us? This is a challenging question for all of us, not just for fourth-grade youngsters. Imagine how we would feel if the pope came to our house for a day. Needless to say, our preparation for his visit would undoubtedly be detailed. We would probably be concerned that everything be as perfect as possible. Yet, when we receive Jesus in Holy Communion, we are visited by someone far greater than the pope. How much greater should be our concern when it is Jesus himself who visits us!

As we have seen, Jesus comes to us in a physical, sacramental way in the Eucharist. He does so in the context of the Holy Sacrifice of the Mass. The liturgy is the most powerful and effective prayer, because it is a prayer not only of the individual speaking to God but of the entire Church speaking to God collectively. First, in the Liturgy of the Word we are fed with the Word of God. Then we move on to the Liturgy of the Eucharist, where we witness the sacred moment of consecration (the transubstantiation of the species of bread and wine), followed by our personal encounter with Jesus in Holy Communion.

We know that in receiving Communion we are receiving a living person, not simply a piece of bread or a mere symbol of Christ. By being eminently aware of Christ's real presence, our devotion is far more fervent than if we regard the Eucharist as a mere symbol. We know, then, that each sacramental encounter with Jesus in Communion makes him *physically* present within us for a short time, that is, *until the host dissolves* and no longer has the "accidents," or physical properties, of bread, such as its chemical structure. But even then Jesus wants to linger on in a spiritual way after the physical presence has ceased. How do we prepare for and respond to that continuing *spiritual* presence?

The *Catechism of the Catholic Church* (1385-1387) gives us some basic guidelines on preparing for Holy Communion. Most importantly, the Church says, we should be in a state of grace. We have already seen that we can stymie the flow of grace by receiving Communion sacrilegiously—in a state of serious, unrepented, and unconfessed sin. Practically, this means that we should examine our conscience and, if we are conscious and certain of any grave or mortal sin which requires the absolution of a priest, we must receive the sacrament of reconciliation beforehand. At the same time, we should repent of any less serious wrongdoing, since these lesser, or venial, sins can hinder to some extent the flow of grace.

Furthermore, the Church requires that we must normally observe a period of at least one hour of fasting before receiving Holy Communion, and that our bodily demeanor (gestures, clothing, and so on) ought to convey the respect, solemnity, and joy of this occasion when Christ becomes our guest. The purpose of this norm is to secure greater reverence for the Blessed Sacrament.

The eucharistic fast that the Church prescribes today is minimal (we should abstain from eating and drinking for one hour before receiving Holy Communion, although abstaining from water and medicine is not required at any time), and these guidelines are a rather recent development. For centuries the Church taught that people should abstain from *all* food and drink, even water, from the preceding midnight, and older Catholics today still have memories of observing this stricter fast. At the same time, many Catholics today personally *choose* to observe a stricter fast as a sign of their respect and devotion for the Blessed Sacrament. This is certainly a worthy practice.

The Church's teaching on the preparation required for Holy Communion is quite basic, and common sense dictates it is appropriate to give even more care and attention to receiving the living God into our hearts than what is prescribed. It is to our advantage to take *special* measures to prepare ourselves for Holy Communion, because the fruit it produces in our lives depends on the disposition with which we receive it. St. Bernard of Clairvaux once remarked, "God will manifest himself to you just as you show yourself available to him." When people complain that they feel like they "receive nothing" when they go to Communion, they are often only betraying their own lack of preparation beforehand.

St. Margaret Mary Alacoque once recounted a vision she had during Mass. In this vision she saw Jesus in the host as the priest was giving Communion. She noticed that Jesus stretched out his arms and seemed eager to be united with some people, while he seemed to enter the mouths of others only because he was being dragged in by cords and bands to which he was bound. Later, our Lord explained the meaning of this vision to St. Margaret Mary. He told her he willingly entered into the hearts of those who were careful to please him and who took pains to prepare themselves beforehand. But he resisted the hearts of others because they were lukewarm Christians who did little in the way of preparation; they had allowed faults and imperfections to permeate their lives with little or no resistance. He explained that he entered the hearts of these people only because of the promises he made when he instituted the sacrament of the Holy Eucharist.

In order to outgrow our minimalist mentality, to learn how to cooperate with God, and to open ourselves up to the abundant graces and fruits available in the Holy Eucharist, we can look for advice to the holy saints who have preceded us. St. Alphonsus Liguori, who is recognized as perhaps the greatest of all moral theologians in the history of the Church, is one good source of practical and sound advice in this area. He himself had a profound devotion to the Eucharist, experienced the real presence of Christ in miraculous ways, and was a renowned teacher of devotion to the Eucharist. In his book on the Blessed Sacrament, *The Holy Eucharist*, he addresses the critical question of how best to prepare ourselves for receiving our Lord Jesus in Holy Communion. He observed sadly that, even though many people were receiving Communion quite frequently, "so many souls after so many Communions make so little advance in the way of God."

Although one Holy Communion is enough to make a person a saint if received with enough love, so few people who receive Communion make major strides toward holiness in doing so. St. Alphonsus recognized that something is wrong with the way in which most persons receive the Eucharist. "The problem," he wrote, "is not in the food. The problem is in the want of due preparation on the part of the communicant." When he studied the lives of the saints, he realized they reaped abundant blessings from their Communions because they took great care in preparing themselves. For example, St. Aloysius Gonzaga devoted three days to preparing himself to receive Holy Communion.

So, let's ask ourselves some questions about how we can prepare ourselves to receive Communion most effectively. How can we maximize our openness to all forms of healing through this sacrament? How do we advance more and more in our *spiritual* lives, thereby experiencing greater spiritual healing? How do we prepare ourselves for our *emotional* healing, so that all the various facets of our personalities might be better integrated? How do we prepare ourselves for our *physical* healing so that our bodies might be healed while receiving the Body of Christ in the Eucharist? How do we incorporate ourselves more perfectly in a societal or communitarian dimension into the Mystical Body of Christ?

The Benefits of Detachment

According to St. Alphonsus Liguori, there are two ways in which we can prepare ourselves. First, he tells us we can do this by being detached from creatures and by driving from our heart everything that is not *of* God and *for* God. He emphasizes this point by telling a story from the life of St. Gertrude.

St. Gertrude asked our Lord what preparation he required of her for Holy Communion. He replied, "I only ask that you come empty of yourself to receive me." What does this mean? It means that everything that captures our attention must be directly or indirectly related to God. If something becomes an end in itself, then it distracts us from God.

For example, television might not be outrightly evil, but it certainly can become a distraction. Today especially, TV has a great potential for instilling a worldly spirit within us. St. Alphonsus recognized that a worldly spirit, in general, is always assailing us. Even though the harried, preoccupied soul may be in a state of grace and, therefore, still be God's friend, the heart can be so overtaken by a worldly spirit there is no room to grow in divine love. We need to detach ourselves from any worldly spirit that does not have a direct relationship with God. (See 1 John 3:7-10).

Jesus said, "For where your treasure is, there also will your heart be" (Mt 6:21, NAB). People who are centered on Christ are not worldly people. They do not dedicate most of their time to superficial reading or television, except to the extent that these things will, at least in some remote way, lead them closer to God. Shopping, making phone calls, and writing letters are all necessary and natural things to do, and there is nothing wrong with these activities. Yet, they can be elevated by the intention behind them. They can become spiritual and prayerful activities that bring us closer to God. How? By remembering that *communing* with God prepares us for *communion* with God. By sharing our lives with God, we develop a yearning for deeper union with him.

In the course of your daily activities, try to imagine Jesus with his arm around your shoulder while you are washing dishes, setting the table, or answering the telephone. Imagine yourself united with Jesus as you perform these activities. Imagine these activities as an extension of that intimate union you experienced with Jesus during your last Holy Communion. Let the living presence of Jesus permeate and sanctify your daily life. By doing so, you will discover that the things of this world become less and less appealing. You will find that the spirit of the world is contaminating you less and less each day. You will find that the prayer of Jesus to his Father in heaven for his disciples at the Last Supper is answered by a change in your own life: "I do not ask that you to take them out of the world but that you keep them from the evil one. They do not belong to the world any more than I belong to the world" (Jn 17:15-16, NAB).

The second recommendation St. Alphonsus makes for preparing ourselves to receive the Body and Blood of Jesus is to stir up "a great desire to receive Jesus Christ and his holy love," with a view of advancing in divine love. He points out that St. Francis de Sales once said, "The principal intention in receiving Communion should be to advance in the love of God." He reminds us that only those who are famishing will receive their fill, and that Jesus came into this world only after people had awaited his coming for many centuries. Therefore, we would not expect him to delight in entering our soul if we have no longing to receive him. In fact, he writes, "It is not becoming that such food should be given to someone who has a loathing for it."

Yet, Jesus does have a great desire to come into our souls. St. Alphonsus quotes Jesus' words to St. Matilda: "No bee flies with such impetuosity to flowers to suck their honey, as I fly to souls in Holy Communion, driven by the vehemence of my love." It is only fitting that we should respond to Jesus' own yearning by our desire to receive him and his divine love in the Eucharist!

We should take great care that we do not go to Communion as just another act within the ceremony of the Mass. We should see it as the tremendous privilege it is, rather than as an obligation. We should desire to receive Jesus with a view to loving him more and advancing in love of God. If fervent love is not present, then something is drastically missing. We should frequently ask ourselves whether the component of love is present in our relationship with Jesus, and most especially in the sacrament of love, the Holy Eucharist.

Looking again at St. Alphonsus' words that "only those who are famishing will receive their fill at this sacred banquet," let us be aware that the ones who are really satisfied, who feel enriched, and who experience healing in their lives are those who truly hunger and yearn for Jesus and not for healing in itself. Remember the blind man who called out, "Jesus, Son of David, have mercy on me." He did not call out, "Jesus, come and heal my blindness." First he acknowledged Jesus as the Messiah. First he sought the Healer. He sought the healing only after Jesus asked him, "What do you want?" We too have to seek the Healer before we seek the healing.

This can be difficult for many people. When people suffer, it is so easy for them to become preoccupied with the pain or with the urgency of the problem. As a result, they focus on the physical, emotional, or spiritual healing and forget about giving glory to God. We need to be sure that our priorities are right. Jesus was a man of great priorities: "Seek *first* the kingdom [of God] and his righteousness, and all these things will be given you besides" (Mt 6:33 NAB, emphasis added). We need to focus primarily on Jesus as a person in the Eucharist, and only then approach him with our own needs, such as healing.

The Importance of Thanksgiving

Just as we should devote adequate time to preparing our hearts before receiving Holy Communion, St. Alphonsus also advises us to spend adequate time in thanksgiving afterward. He once told the story about a priest who spotted a man leaving church immediately after Communion. The priest summoned the altar boys, gave them lighted candles, and sent them to accompany the man home. "What's the matter?" the man asked. "Oh," said the boys, "we were sent to accompany our Lord, who is still present in your heart."

St. Alphonsus observes that there is "no prayer more dear to God than that which is made after Holy Communion." In those days, he noticed that many people devoted themselves to spiritual reading after receiving Communion. He recommended instead that people use this time for conversing with Jesus, who is within us. He went on to say that the "devout acts of love which we then make have greater merit in the sight of God than those which we make at other times, because they are then animated by the presence of Jesus Christ, who is united to our souls."

We may spend one, two, or three hours in devout prayer, and our prayer is certainly holy and pleasing to God. Yet, when we spend one, two, or three minutes in fervent prayer right after receiving Holy Communion, our prayer may be more beneficial than several hours of fervent prayer without that sacramental presence. The power of the presence of Jesus gives life to our post-Communion prayer. It is precisely for this reason that it is so important to make the Eucharist the core of our prayer life. When we do this, we will then have the faith to seek healing when Jesus asks us, "What do you wish?" Then, healing is recognized as pertinent but secondary. The primary purpose is union with God and giving glory to him.

St. Teresa of Avila, one of the greatest mystics of the Church, was an exemplary model of Christlike charity and humility. In her writings we find that God gave St. Teresa mystical insights regarding Holy Communion, indicating to her that Christ remains spiritually present in a person's *soul* after he is no longer physically present in a person's body. Physically Jesus remains in a person's body for perhaps five, ten, or fifteen minutes after receiving Communion, until the host dissolves and no longer has the chemical structure of bread. At that point, Christ is no longer physically present in the person. But St. Teresa of Avila pointed out that spiritually Christ remains in a person's soul for much longer, "as on a throne of grace, asking the person, 'What would you have me do for you? I have come from heaven on purpose to grant you graces; ask what you will, as much as you will, and you will be heard.'" That revelation highlights the importance of devotion as an "afterglow" of receiving this august sacrament. This recognized "spiritual" presence was the rationale in an earlier time (when people could receive Communion only once a month) for the practiced custom of spending two weeks preparing for Communion and two weeks in thanksgiving after Communion.

Other saints have also stressed the importance of devoting adequate time to thanksgiving after Communion. St. John Chrysostom noted that when we enjoy a delicious meal at a banquet, we savor every morsel and refuse anything bitter afterward so we will not lose the sweet flavor of the food we so thoroughly enjoyed. He advises us, therefore, to take great care not to lose the heavenly flavor of the Body of Jesus Christ by turning to the cares of the world too soon.

"When the merchants of India have brought home their precious porcelain," St. Francis de Sales wrote, "they are very careful in conveying it to their storehouses lest they should stumble and break their costly wares. In like manner should the Christian, when he carries the priceless treasure of our Lord's Body, walk with great care and circumspection in order not to lose the costly gift committed to his keeping."

What, then, constitutes a good thanksgiving? We should complete our union with Jesus by sincerely offering ourselves to him. Nothing can be more intimate than the union that takes place between the Creator and his creatures in Communion. If we stop a moment to think about it, it is a mystery that baffles thought: the Son of God comes into our hearts under the appearance of bread and wine. The Creator has humbled himself to enter the hearts and souls of his creatures. Whereas we would normally proclaim, "How great is the Lord and greatly to be praised," our natural response might now be to say, "How small is the Lord and greatly to be loved."

The immense love that Jesus has for us should be the focus of our attention. But Jesus' love for us should evoke, in turn, our love for him. Love must be mutual to produce union. We must return love for love. Out of his love for us and our love for him, we then can offer him the only thing we have to offer him, and what he values most: our hearts. There is nothing more pleasing to Jesus than a person who is determined to serve him. If we offer ourselves to him to do as he pleases, to serve him with all the fervor we can, to avoid sin, and to accept the bitter and the sweet that come our way, then our Communion will really be just that—a union with God.

The second element of our thanksgiving after Communion is a time of petition. Our first and foremost petition should be that God will grant us the grace to fulfill everything we have promised to him in offering ourselves to him. At the same time, we can really take advantage of—in a good sense—the beneficence of Jesus in our soul. As St. Teresa reminds us, he is there as a king reigning in our hearts, offering to grant us whatever we seek that conforms with his will.

We need to remember this when we receive him in Holy

Communion. He is present within us and is asking us, "What do you want?" Are we just going to shuffle away and not do anything? Are we just going to swallow the host and do nothing more? This is a time to give Jesus our love and our faith. To trust him. To ask him what we want to ask him and let him heal us.

Indeed, Jesus wants more for us than we want for ourselves! Do we want to be saved? Jesus wants to save us more than we want to be saved. Do we want to be forgiven? Jesus wants to forgive us more than we want to be forgiven. Do we want to be healed? Jesus wants to heal us far more than we want to be healed. If we do not receive salvation, forgiveness, or healing, it is not due to a lack on Jesus' part; it is due to some obstacle we have placed in the way. We must be on the alert not to allow obstacles like worldliness and distractions to block his path.

It takes some persons a lifetime to learn the simple fact that God, in his loving compassion, wants more good for us than we want for ourselves. We need to learn to respond to God, because he is there, ready to respond to us. We need to ask in order to receive. We need to abide in him, so that he abides in us. As I pointed out in my book *When God Says No: 25 Reasons Why Some Prayers Are Not Answered*, the obstacles to successful prayer of petition come from us and not from God.

A third element that should characterize our thanksgiving after Communion is praise. Jesus is present within us in the temples of our hearts. We are carrying Jesus, the Incarnate Son of God, in our hearts. Songs of praise and rejoicing should welcome him. As an example, we need only to recall Mary's song of praise and rejoicing when she was carrying Jesus in her womb:

My soul proclaims the greatness of the Lord;
my spirit rejoices in God my savior.
For he has looked upon his handmaid's lowliness;
behold, from now on will all ages call me blessed.
The Mighty One has done great things for me,
and holy is his name.

LUKE 1:46-49, NAB

Although nothing in Mary's outward appearance distinguished her from other pregnant women, in the depths of her heart she was living out the closest possible union between God and one of his creatures. She was a living tabernacle where the Holy of Holies was residing. Unceasingly she prayed that she might adore the Word made Flesh within her, that she might be united more closely with God and be transformed by his love, and that she might join in offering continual praise, which is the only homage worthy of the almighty and omnipotent God. When we receive the living Jesus into our hearts at Holy Communion, we too become temples of the living God and share in this prayer of Mary. We should strive to live in this spirit of continual adoration of the Trinity dwelling within our soul.

We have a lot to look forward to! Through the Eucharist, Jesus is giving us a foretaste of the banquet he has prepared for us in heaven. Are we enjoying it, or are we simply skipping through it? Are we simply blundering our way through all these precious treasures? Are we like an infant who has inherited a billion dollars but does not know it and cannot spend it? Are we in possession of a treasure that holds no meaning because of our own immaturity in coping and dealing with it?

Are we appreciative and thankful for God's gift to us? Are we bursting with gratitude for this greatest of gifts? To facilitate our response, it is good to recall again and again that provocative statement used by St. Augustine in the fourth century: "The only thing God does not know is how he could possibly give us a gift greater than himself."

SIX

Healing in the Eucharistic Assembly

Jesus Christ, who died, who was raised from the dead, who is seated at the right hand of God, and who intercedes for us, is present in many ways in his Church. Indeed, the *Catechism of the Catholic Church* (1373) summarizes the ways in which Jesus is present in his Church.

Jesus is present in his Word; it is he himself who speaks to us whenever we read the sacred Scriptures or hear them proclaimed. In Matthew 25:31-46, Jesus tells us he is also present in the poor, the sick, and the imprisoned whom he has entrusted to our care. Jesus gave us the seven sacraments, in each of which he is present in a special way conferring his grace upon us. Jesus also told us he is present whenever we gather with others to praise and worship him: "For where two or three are gathered together in my name, there am I in the midst of them" (Mt 18:20, NAB).

Of those occasions when we gather with others to praise and worship God, the sacrifice of the Mass surpasses them all. When Christians come together to celebrate the Mass, Christ himself is at its head, presiding over every celebration, with the bishop or priest representing him. And as we have already seen, Christ is present to each and every one of us individually in receiving the eucharistic species. But he is also present in the prayerful assembled community. The earthly liturgy we celebrate at Mass is but a foretaste of the heavenly liturgy that awaits us.

For this reason, it is important to examine the Mass more closely. Since our eucharistic encounter with Christ generally occurs within the context of the liturgical celebration with other believers, the Eucharist is not only a one-to-one encounter but a societal encounter, where God's transforming power is available to us both individually and corporately.

The *Instruction on the Worship of the Eucharistic Mystery* (3a), which was a fruit of the Second Vatican Council, reminds us that the Mass, even in its communitarian aspect, has four dimensions:

The Mass is a sacrifice. It is the sacrifice of Calvary reenacted, but *not repeated*, because Hebrews 9:27 tells us Christ died once and he can die no more. It is a symbolic reenactment of the death of Christ, but not a real death. There is a real Person present after the consecration, but not a real death. It is a sacrifice because of the words of consecration that Jesus used: "This is my body, which will be *given* for you...; this is my blood which will be *shed* for you." It is a sacrifice because Paul says in 1 Corinthians 11:26 (NAB), "For as often as you eat this bread and drink the cup, you *proclaim the death of the Lord* until he comes" (emphasis added). This is why we refer to the Mass as the Holy *Sacrifice* of the Mass. Many people do not like to refer to the Mass in this way because they would prefer to downplay the sacrificial element. But Scripture tells us otherwise in at least three places, and it is reaffirmed by Vatican II (*The Constitution on the Sacred Liturgy*, 47).

It is interesting to note that the word "host," which is often used to refer to the Blessed Sacrament, comes from our belief that the Mass is a true and unbloody renewal of Calvary on our altars. It is derived from the Latin word *hostia*, meaning victim. The victim, of course, is Jesus Christ. He was offered on the altar of the cross for our salvation; today the consecrated bread is changed into Christ's real presence, the sacramental presence of the Victim slain for our sins. It was during the Middle Ages that the word "host" was used to refer to the consecrated altar breads used in Communion and exposed for the adoration of the faithful.

The Mass is a meal. Every time we go to Mass, we are attending a communal meal, and we often refer to this meal as the Lord's Supper. The first Mass was also a meal, the Passover meal; we commonly refer to it as the Last Supper. The words that were spoken then and now are "Take and eat...; take and drink...." This leaves no doubt that the Mass is a meal in which we consume food and beverage and derive sustenance from them. However, this is a meal like no other meal, because it is a foretaste of the eternal banquet that heaven offers.

The Mass is a memorial. Jesus instructed us, "Do this in memory of me" (Lk 22:19). We no longer celebrate this meal as the Passover meal in memory of Moses, the great rescuer of the Israelites. At the Last Supper Passover meal, Jesus proclaimed that henceforth it was to be celebrated in memory of himself, the new Rescuer, the new Redeemer, who was to perform the redeeming act a few hours later on Good Friday. A short prayer that immediately follows the consecration, called the Anamnesis ("Remembrance") Prayer, refers to this memorial dimension.

The Mass is an act of thanksgiving. In early Greek, the word *eucharistia*, from which we get the word Eucharist, means *good gift*. In later Greek it meant, by connotation, *thanksgiving for a good gift*. Jesus took the bread, broke it, and *gave thanks* (Lk 22:19). That is, he said grace. In the Mass, we give thanks to God for his many favors in the prophetic spirit of the psalmist: "I will lift up the cup of salvation ... I will sacrifice a thank offering in the presence of all his people" (see Ps 116:13-18).

Thus we have the four elements that characterize the Mass: a sacrifice, a meal, a memorial, and a thanksgiving. Using these four elements, we can construct a definition: "The Mass is a sacrificial, memorial meal of thanksgiving." If we omit any one of these four elements, a dimension of eucharistic spirituality is missing. Such an omission would also violate the theology of the Eucharist as described by the Council of Trent and the Second Vatican Council. By recognizing all four elements and capitalizing upon them in our own spiritual life, we are maximizing the effects of the Eucharist, both in terms of personal sanctification and in terms of physical and emotional healing. With this very minimal amount of catechetical knowledge, and with enough good will to bring about devotion or fervor (which is responding to grace), we have all we need to enhance our physical, emotional, and spiritual lives in the fullest way possible. For this reason, the Eucharist is the most effective means of healing known to mankind.

Touching the Healer in the Eucharist

We all know there are many ways in which healing can occur. For example, many people are healed when they are anointed with holy oil, particularly in the sacrament of the anointing of the sick. "Is anyone among you sick? He should summon the presbyters of the church, and they should pray over him and anoint [him] with oil in the name of the Lord, and the prayer of faith will save the sick person, and the Lord will raise him up. If he has committed any sins, he will be forgiven" (Jas 5:14-15, NAB). We also know that many people are healed through the laying on of hands. Jesus said, "These signs will accompany those who believe...; they will lay hands on the sick, and they will recover" (Mk 16:17-18).

In Matthew 8:5-13 and in Luke 7:1-10, we see how Jesus healed the centurion's servant without being physically present with the boy, and he exorcised the daughter of the Canaanite woman from a distance (see Matthew 15:22-28 and Mark 7:25-30). Remarkably, if we have deep faith in Jesus, we are empowered to heal just as he did (see John 14:12).

Nonetheless, in spite of the avenues of healing by anointing, laying on of hands, prayers of petition, and intercession, healing through the Eucharist is by far the greatest way healing can occur. The Eucharist is a healing sacrament because, in receiving this sacrament, we are touching Jesus, the Healer himself, and he is touching us. If we fail to focus on Christ, and if this focus is not a primary dynamic in our spiritual life, our prayer will be flaccid and inefficacious. To understand this spiritual principle, we need only to recall the episode in Matthew 14:22-26 and Mark 6:45-56, when the disciples left Jesus on the shore to pray one evening, while they went on ahead of him to Bethsaida in their boat. In the middle of the night, they saw Jesus walking toward them on the sea and were terrified. "It is a ghost," they cried out in fear. But Jesus reassured them: "Take courage, it is I; do not be afraid."

The passage in Matthew recounts how Peter then said, "Lord, if it is you, command me to come to you on the water." So Jesus commanded him to come. Peter stepped out of the boat and walked on the water, just as he saw Jesus do. He was fine until a squall suddenly set the water into a turbulence. Realizing how strong the wind was, he became frightened and began to sink. He took his eyes off Jesus; he was no longer focused on Christ. He focused on the problem rather than on the problem-solver. As a result, he began to sink. Jesus reached down and pulled him back to the surface of the water with a handclasp. "O you of little faith! Why did you doubt?" he asked.

When we take our eyes off Jesus, and when we stop having that Christ-centered focus in our spirituality—especially in our eucharistic spirituality—we will find ourselves swamped with the churning waters of our problems. Consequently, we become far more concerned with our problems than with encountering the One who can solve them. It is so difficult to "seek first the kingdom of God" and to focus on the Lord when we are preoccupied with our petty little problems. We learn from this passage in Matthew that we must make it our priority to focus on Christ rather than looking at the waves, the turbulence, and the issues of life around us. The easiest way to focus on and encounter him is by a personal devotion to him in the Eucharist.

Jesus says, "Come to me all you who labor and are burdened, and I will give you rest" (Mt 11:28, NAB). Do we accept this invitation? Do we really come to him? There are many ways we can come to Jesus, such as through prayer. But to come to him in a personal, physical, and sacramental way, and at the same time to encounter him in his corporate presence in the liturgical assembly, is something totally different. Every time we celebrate Mass together and receive Holy Communion, we are coming to Jesus in these very special ways. This is the premiere form of encountering Christ, the form with remarkable effects. We should cultivate these forms of union with him in a devout way, lest the Mass become ritualistic, routine, or mechanical. We have to be on guard that our eucharistic devotion does not deteriorate. Indeed, we must make every effort to preserve a union with the Healer in which healing can take place in the ambience of his love, *within* us and *among* us.

This means learning how to relax in God's arms, or in the words of Jesus, "to abide" in him. He abides in us when he comes into our hearts at Communion. But do we abide in him? Do we relax in his arms? Do we let ourselves be hugged into holiness and wholeness? All we have to do is surrender in *love*.

It can be said that, in some way, this Eucharistic liturgy is the answer to all of life's problems. We can encounter love in its most pristine form in Jesus—love personified in the assembly spiritually, and in Communion physically, the one who loves the Father and who is beloved by the Father. Let us remember Jesus' promise to us: "As the Father has loved me, so have I loved you; *abide in my love*" (Jn 15:9, RSV, emphasis added). Jesus communicates God's love to us through his humanity as well as his divinity. When we encounter him, we also encounter the Father (see John 14:7-10) and the Holy Spirit (see John 14:16-17). We are immersed in the very heart of the Trinity, in the very heart of God. "God is love, and he who abides in love abides in God, and God abides in him" (1 Jn 4:16, RSV).

SEVEN

Jesus' Corporate Healing Presence

When pondering our personal encounter with Jesus in the Eucharist at Mass, we should not lose sight of the fact that the Eucharist is also a *societal* encounter where God's transforming power is available to us *corporately* as alluded to in the previous chapter. The Christian community can be compared to burning coals. When separated from each other, one after the other is easily extinguished. But when gathered together, the fire of one tends to preserve that of another, and the glowing coals sometimes ignite others that would otherwise remain unlit.

Jesus' own love should burn in the hearts of the faithful. This is the core of his words to us, "Abide in my love." St. Paul prayed for the "abiding" spiritual presence within the worshiping community when he wrote: "May the God of endurance and encouragement grant you to think in harmony with one another, *in keeping with Christ Jesus*, that *with one accord* you may with one voice glorify the God and Father of our Lord Jesus Christ" (Rom 15:5-6, NAB, emphasis added). Jesus' "abiding" presence in a worshiping community was first manifested right after his resurrection in the eucharistic "breaking of the bread" with the disciples at Emmaus as recounted in Luke 24.

But true Christian community is not just a crowd of people or a juxtaposition of bodies. The group must be gathered "in his name" in a dynamic of loving concord in order for Christ to truly dwell in that group. In 2 Corinthians 6:15-16 (NAB), Paul points out the need *not just for assembling* but also for *loving harmony* among believers, who constitute "the temple of the living God." And to excite the expectancy of God's communitarian presence, he quotes the Lord's promise in Leviticus 26:12: "And I will walk among you, and will be your God, and you shall be my people" (RSV). This kind of unity is essential to Christian gatherings, especially among people who are looking for Jesus' presence to be manifested in divine healings.

In Old Testament times, King David took special delight in glorifying God in the assembly gathered together for worship. The many psalms, or religious songs, he composed attest to this great joy. Addressing the God who is enthroned in the praises of his people, David sings, "In the midst of the assembly I will praise you" (Ps 22:22b). He proclaims his resolve to exalt God in the congregation in Psalm 57:10b: "I will chant your praise among the nations."

The author of the Epistle to the Hebrews quotes David's psalm: "I will proclaim your name to my brothers, in the midst of the assembly I will praise you" (Heb 2:12, NAB). In doing so, he puts this pericope into a New Testament context, presumably at a gathering where the Eucharist is being celebrated.

The promise of the Lord's presence among his people is fulfilled each time the congregation joins together in doctrinal "harmony" by faith. The Holy Sacrifice of the Mass is the perfect gathering to "continually offer God a sacrifice of praise, that is, the fruit of lips that confess his name" (Heb 13:15, NAB). This is particularly true when praise of God is "harmonized" in music, for as St. Augustine said, "He who sings prays twice." God's word urges us to "sing to the Lord a new song of praise *in the assembly of the faithful*" (Ps 149:1), as well as to "praise the Lord in his sanctuary" (Ps 150:1).

Scripture also tells us this harmony in music is a two-way street: "The Lord, your God, is in your midst.... He will sing joyfully because of you" (Zep 3:17, NAB). Hence, St. Paul urges us to sing "psalms, hymns, and spiritual songs with gratitude in your hearts to God" (Col 3:16; see also Ephesians 5:19 and James 5:13). It is significant that Paul makes two references to joining together in song "with thankful hearts" or "in gratitude," in light of the fact the Greek word *eucharistia* means thanksgiving.

Jeremiah reminds us that the Lord "clings" to his people as a whole (and not just as individual persons) for praise and honor (see Jeremiah 13:11). When he is praised and honored in a devout and worshipful Mass, his presence becomes the focus which effects the exercise of his healing power among his people. In the words of the *Instruction on the Worship of the Eucharistic Mystery* (3c, 3d), "The celebration of the Eucharist which takes place at Mass is the action not only of Christ, but also of the Church.... Hence no Mass, indeed no liturgical action, is a purely private action."

Corporate Healing in the Liturgy

There are four forms in which God is present in the liturgy, all of which can effect healing in the community. These four forms are listed in the Vatican II document *The Constitution on the Sacred Liturgy* (7), as enumerated here:

1. In the prayerful gathering itself (see Matthew 18:20; Eph 2:20-22);
2. In the Christic priestly presence, both in the priest and in the community of lay people gathered in his name (see 1 Peter 2:5);
3. In the publicly proclaimed Word of God (see Hebrews 4:12; John 15:7);
4. In the eucharistic species—the consecrated elements —not just in themselves but also as the sacrament nucleates the community in worship (see 1 Corinthians 10:17).

The last form of presence has not just a corporal but a *corporate* healing dimension, at least *preventively*, when received in a worthy manner (nonsacrilegiously), as implied in 1 Corinthians 11:30, NAB: "That is why many among you are ill and infirm, and a considerable number are dying." (Note the plurality of "many among you" and "a considerable number.") Likewise, there is an inference in 10:17 of a corporate healing—a healing or prevention of spiritual disunity among communicants: "Because the loaf of bread is one, we, though many, are one body, for we all partake of the one loaf."

Another point of reference for the corporate healing presence is based on the two dimensions of the Mass (the Liturgy of the Word and the Liturgy of the Eucharist). They each provide, as it were, an *ambience* for a healing encounter. The first provides an encounter with the revealed Word, and the second is an encounter with the Revealer. Jesus hints at both encounters (with revealed and Revealer) in John 15:7: "If you remain in *me* and *my words* remain in you, ask for whatever you want and it will be done for you" (emphasis added). There is once again another intimation of both encounters in Revelation 3:20: "Behold, I stand at the door and knock. If anyone *hears my voice* and opens the door, [then] *I* will enter his house and dine *with him,* and he *with me....*"

There are many scriptural references related to the Lord's presence as it effects healing or health. For instance, Psalm 91:9-10 (emphasis added) says: "You have the Lord for *your refuge;* you have made the Most High your stronghold. No evil shall befall you, nor affliction come near your tent." And Ephesians 3:20 (NIV) tells us that Christ "is able to do immeasurably more than all we ask or imagine, according to his *power* that is at work *within us*" (emphasis added). This power, especially his healing power, is particularly present during his post-Communion presence in us.

If our Communion prayers are devout, he dwells within our hearts through faith (see Ephesians 3:17), but also through love, as St. John tells us: "Whoever remains in love remains in God and God in him" (1 Jn 4:16, NAB). Furthermore, if we love one another (as in a love-united liturgical assembly), "God remains in us, and his love is brought to perfection in us" (1 Jn 4:12).

To foster this divine corporate presence, St. Paul urges all the believers to be lovingly united in the goal of worshiping the Lord: "If there is any encouragement in Christ, any solace in love, any participation in the Spirit, any compassion and mercy, complete my joy by being of the same mind, with the same love, *united in heart, thinking one thing*" (Phil 2:1-2, NAB, emphasis added). In 2 Corinthians 13:11, St. Paul reminds us about the gift that awaits those believers who are united to each other in their love of God: "Finally, brothers, rejoice. Mend your ways, encourage one another, agree with one another, live in peace and the God of love and peace will be with you" (NAB). When a liturgical gathering fosters loving unity while worshiping the God of unity, marvelous healings can occur.

St. John articulated this idea of Jesus' presence among us this way: "And his commandment is this: we should believe in the name of his Son, Jesus Christ, and love one another just as he commanded us. Those who keep his commandments remain in him, and he in them, and the way we know that he remains in us is from the Spirit that he gave us" (1 Jn 3:23-24, NAB). Hence, when believers, who like St. Paul "live by faith in the Son of God" (Gal 2:20), are joined together as an authentic community of expectant faith and are filled with his love, then that divine healing love is powerfully present. As St. Paul asserts, "Christ is not weak toward you but powerful in you" (2 Cor 13:3, NAB).

Just as physical healings tend to occur when the *physical* presence or touch of Christ is experienced in Holy Communion, so also spiritual healings may be expected when there is a *spiritual* encounter with the healing Christ in the eucharistic assembly. This is true even "where two or three are gathered together" in Christ's name (Mt 18:20, NAB). This is reminiscent of the Lord's promise to Moses: "An altar of earth you shall make for me, and upon it you shall sacrifice your holocausts and peace offerings, your sheep and your oxen. In whatever place I choose for the remembrance of my name *I will come to you and bless you*" (Ex 20:24, NAB, emphasis added).

The Lord wants to bless us especially with spiritual healings, which are sought less but needed more than physical healings. Spiritual healings can assume a wide variety of forms, such as deliverance from forces of evil, conquering sinful habits, curing aridity in prayer, the healing of turbulent marriages, and overcoming resistance to deep, grace-flooded repentance, etc.

St. Paul prayed for the Ephesians that God would "grant you in accord with the riches of his glory to be strengthened with *power* through his Spirit in the inner self, and that Christ may dwell in your hearts through faith" (Eph 3:16-17, emphasis added). But just as the strength (health) and the strengthening (healing) of a human body require a metabolism in which all the biochemical components work harmoniously together, so also the spiritual health and healing of an assembled body of the faithful—and of its individual members—are subject to the norms of divine harmonics.

A good example is that of an orchestra. In a pre-concert warm up, the random playing of instruments by the orchestra produces only a raucous cacophony, not euphony. It is only when the conductor taps his or her baton on the podium and directs all the musicians in an orchestrated harmony or "symphony" that the musical talents of all are optimally used. In this analogy we can see why St. Paul urged the Corinthians, and also the Philippians, to live in "harmony" as a Christian community. The only way to ensure optimal healing effects is to have all the participants follow the guiding presence of the Divine Conductor, Jesus. *His healing power is evidenced only in an atmosphere of unity and loving concord.* That is why the early Christians witnessed so many healing miracles during their eucharistic assemblies.

Miraculous Power in the Early Church

The history of those flurries of awesome miracles and healings that occurred in the early Christian liturgies due to the Lord's spiritual presence is recorded in the Acts of the Apostles. As we review this history in the following scriptural quotations, let us immerse ourselves imaginatively in the kind of Christian community they experienced, and compare it with the typical parish of our time. The stark comparison may help us understand why so few healings occur during today's eucharistic liturgies (referred to in Scripture as the "breaking of the bread").

St. Luke tells us:

They devoted themselves to the teaching of the apostles and to the communal life, to the breaking of the bread and to the prayers. Awe came upon everyone, and many *wonders and signs* were done through the apostles. All who believed were together and had all things in common; they would sell their property and possessions and divide them among all according to each one's need. Every day they devoted themselves to meeting together in the temple area and to breaking bread in their homes. They ate their meals with exultation and sincerity of heart, praising God and enjoying favor with all the people. And every day the Lord added to their number those who were being saved.

ACTS 2:42-47, NAB, emphasis added

Again, St. Luke recounts the powerful presence of God among those who worshiped him:

As they prayed, the place where they were gathered shook, and they were all filled with the Holy Spirit and continued to speak the word of God with boldness. The community of believers was of one heart and mind, and no one claimed that any of his possessions was his own, but they had everything in common. With great power the apostles bore witness to the resurrection of the Lord Jesus, *and great favor was accorded them all.* There was no needy person among them.

ACTS 4:31-34, NAB, emphasis added

Other instances of the early believers' experiencing miraculous signs are recorded in the Gospels. Truly, the Lord, who had promised to be with them "always, until the end of the age" (Mt 28:20, NAB), fulfilled that promise as he "worked with them and confirmed the word through accompanying signs" (Mk 16:20). And this must have led them to anticipate an even deeper presence of God—one that would confer a permanent healing of *all* disease and disorder—*after* the end of the age.

The Bible says that this will be the time of the "new age" when the New Jerusalem will come down from heaven, when the voice from the throne will announce, "Behold, God's dwelling is with the human race. He will dwell with them and they will be his people and God himself will always be with them [as their God]. He will wipe every tear from their eyes, and there shall be no more death or mourning, wailing or pain, [for] the old order has passed away" (Rv 21:3-4, NAB).

From meditating on the excerpts from the Acts of the Apostles, we can see how the Lord delights in his people and rewards those who gather in loving unity to praise and worship him. As the psalmist wrote in addressing the Lord, "Toward the faithful you are faithful" (Ps 18:26, NAB). God's miracles and wonders are for those who would avail themselves of these gifts of his loving compassion. We neglect them to our own disadvantage.

When we encounter Jesus physically and sacramentally in the Eucharist, we can learn experientially what it means to abide in him and to have him abide in us. Let us aim to do this at all times, but particularly when attending Mass and receiving Jesus in Holy Communion. And let us continue to abide in his love through our whole day and our whole week, until we are next refreshed with the Bread of Heaven during that banquet of love. Our corporate communion is but a foretaste of the banquet he has prepared for us ultimately in heaven (see Luke 22:30).

EIGHT

The Healing Power of the Eucharist

In 1 Thessalonians 5:23, St. Paul speaks about three parts of the human personality: "May the God of peace himself make you perfectly holy and may you entirely, *spirit, soul, and body,* be preserved blameless for the coming of our Lord Jesus Christ" (NAB, emphasis added). In other translations, this tripartite division of spirit, soul, and body is rendered as body, mind, and spirit. These are the three major areas in which human beings can suffer from wounds, and the three dimensions of the human personality where God's healing action can take place.

Two areas are self-explanatory, and the damage that can occur to them is rather evident. The body, of course, refers to our physical body. Our bodies can suffer from a congenital defect, be ravaged by disease, or be injured in an accident. When this happens, some type of healing is needed for the body to recover. Likewise with the mind. We are all familiar with the psychological illnesses that can affect a person's mind and the many therapies available for such disorders. Many people, however, do not recognize that we human beings are subject to spiritual disorders—those that disturb our relationship with God in grace and prayer.

In the realm of our spirit, two types of defect can occur which call for some type of healing. The first type of spiritual defect is an intrinsic spiritual disorder that consists of a kind of "soul-soiling" which we call a state of sin—either grievous or minor (see 1 John 5:17)—or habits of sin (see 1 John 3:6). The second type of spiritual defect is an extrinsic spiritual disorder that occurs as the result of demonic attacks from outside the soul. These demonic forces are the works of the devil or his minions—demons and evil spirits that work against our spiritual welfare. The "Our Father" (or the Lord's Prayer) refers to both of these spiritual forces, intrinsic and extrinsic. When we pray the petition, "Forgive us our trespasses," we are asking God to free us from the intrinsic spiritual disorders that have occurred because we have yielded to sin. When we pray the last petition in the prayer, "Deliver us from evil," we are asking God to protect us from the extrinsic spiritual disorders that can be brought on by attacks of the evil one from outside. It is from this last petition that we get the term "deliverance prayer," which is a kind of minor exorcism.

When we thus examine the realm of the human spirit (soul), we can conclude there are not three but four types of disorder that require, correspondingly, four types of healing: physical; emotional; intrinsic spiritual healing, which is healing from sin; and extrinsic spiritual healing, in which demonic forces are dispelled. Moreover, as we shall show, all four types of healing are eminently available through the Eucharist. Clearly it follows that a smorgasbord of healing benefits is available to us through the healing power of the Eucharist.

Healing for Body, Mind, and Spirit

The popular definition of health is the condition of being sound in body, mind, and spirit. This clearly implies freedom from disease and pain, and it also implies the fullness of the vitality of life. Sickness, of course, impairs our vital functions and diminishes our life forces. When a person looks sick, or as we sometimes say, "half-alive" or "like death warmed over," we know this person needs more "life" or vitality—the purpose of all forms of healing. Yet Jesus promised, "I came so that they might have *life* and have it more abundantly" (Jn 10:10, emphasis added). Jesus offers us abundant life, the fullness of life. The fullness of life that he offers is fullness of physical life, emotional life, and spiritual life—healing in body, mind, and spirit.

As we have already seen, Jesus has revealed to us that this fullness of life, which is health in the broadest sense, is preeminently conferred through the Eucharist: "The one who feeds on me will have *life* because of me" (Jn 6:57, NAB, emphasis added). We have already seen too that Jesus' words imply a habitual and frequent action: Whoever feeds on him, that is, nourished by Communion habitually or frequently, will have life.

Think of how we are nourished physically. The food that we ate last week satisfied our hunger at the time. Even though that satisfaction is now gone, that food has become part of the continuous process of nourishment, keeping our bodies alive. On one hand, that food had a temporary effect: It satisfied our hunger. On the other hand, though, it also has an ongoing effect: It is keeping our bodies alive. Just as we have to feed our bodies repeatedly to sustain physical life, so too we have to repeatedly feed on Christ to sustain our spiritual life. This is why Jesus uses the word "feeds" in John 6:57. He is reminding us that we have to receive him frequently and habitually in Communion and not simply consume his Body and Blood once. Unlike baptism, this is not a one-time sacrament.

The important point to remember is that receiving Communion is very different in its healing function than the spiritual prayer for healing we say over an individual. The Eucharist is not merely some abstract, spiritual contact with Jesus. In the Eucharist we have direct physical contact with Jesus. Why is this so important? When we study the Gospel accounts of people being healed, we discover a notable fact: We see that everyone who touched Jesus was healed if they touched him with expectant faith. Matthew 14:35-36 (NAB) tells us, "People brought to him all those who were sick and begged him that they might touch only the tassel on his cloak, and as many as touched it were healed." In the Eucharist, we touch Jesus and Jesus touches us.

In John 6:56 (RSV) Jesus says, "He who eats my flesh and drinks my blood abides in me, and I in him." The Greek word for abide is *meno*. This was one of St. John's favorite words; he uses it in ten places in his Gospel. The word *meno* means to remain intimately present to, to be nestled into, to be grafted into. It conveys a very deep sense of intimacy, and in no way signifies a temporary encounter. Even though our encounter with Jesus in the Eucharist is temporary, the effect is lasting. We are grafted into Christ and we are united with him, like branches united to the vine (see John 15:4).

In the Liturgy of the Eucharist, several prayers at Communion time refer to the healing power of the Eucharist. For instance, immediately after the Lord's Prayer, the priest says the following prayer (italics added): "Deliver us, Lord, *from every evil*, and *grant us peace in our day*. In your mercy keep us *free from sin* and protect us *from all anxiety* as we wait in joyful hope for the coming of our Savior, Jesus Christ." Upon closer examination, it becomes apparent that this simple prayer encompasses several distinct forms of healing. First of all, the priest prays a prayer of deliverance, so that we might all be healed of any extrinsic spiritual disorders that occur from the attacks of demonic forces. This is based on 1 Corinthians 10:21 (RSV): "You cannot partake of the [eucharistic] table of the Lord and of the table of demons." Secondly, he prays for societal or communitarian healing (i.e., peace that heals interpersonal or intrapersonal conflict). Thirdly, he prays for the healing of our intrinsic spiritual disorders, asking God to free us from our state of sin. Finally, he prays for our emotional healing, freedom from anxiety and guilt feelings so we can experience inner peace and joyful hope.

Later on, the priest has the option of reciting another prayer that speaks about physical healing (body) and emotional healing (mind) as he prepares to receive Holy Communion himself (italics added): "Lord Jesus Christ, with faith in your love and mercy I eat your body and drink your blood. Let it not bring me condemnation, *but health in mind and body*."

Finally, there is a prayer that the congregation recites before approaching the altar to receive Holy Communion: "Lord, I am not worthy to receive you, but only say the word and I shall be *healed*." This prayer has its origins in the story about the healing of a centurion's servant in Matthew 8:5-13. In faith, he knew that Jesus needed only to say the word for his servant to be healed. "And Jesus said to the centurion, 'You may go; as you have believed, let it be done for you'" (Mt. 8:13, NAB).

Our prayer before Communion, then, is a paraphrase of the centurion's words. When we pray, "...but only say the word and I shall be healed," we are, in some way, replicating the healing faith of that centurion. If our spirit echoes that blessed assurance, "I shall be healed," and if we do not merely mouth the words, then this simple prayer of expectancy can educe some astonishing results in terms of bodily healing, emotional integration, and spiritual growth.

In Acts 2:42 (NAB), we read that the early Christians "devoted themselves to the teaching of the apostles and to the communal life, to the breaking of the bread and to the prayers." It is noteworthy that they did not simply *participate* in these activities, including the Eucharist (the "breaking of bread"), but *devoted* themselves to them. The word *devoted* has several connotations and says much about the expectant faith of those early Christians, especially as they approached Jesus in the sacrament of the Eucharist. And as we have already seen in a previous chapter, it is equally noteworthy that their devotion had a corporate dimension and was a truly communitarian experience: the whole community had this surging expectancy of faith because they all believed that they were to experience a real encounter with Jesus himself. The fullness of life which Jesus confers on us through the Eucharist is not due to following the ritual but because of him: "The one who feeds on me will have life *because of me*" (Jn 6:57, NAB, emphasis added).

Expectant Fervor in the Early Church

The Holy Sacrifice of the Mass had basically the same structure in the early Church as it has today. Before being fed with the Body and Blood of Christ in the Liturgy of the Eucharist, the congregation was fed with the Word of God in the Liturgy of the Word. During this first part of the Mass, they would listen to readings from the Old Testament and from the epistles. Then, before the public proclamation from the gospels, which contain the only direct quotations from Jesus, they would stand as a sign of respect and sing the Great Alleluia.

The early Christians had tremendous expectancy in their faith. They could hardly wait for the words of the Gospel to be proclaimed. They were so intent on this part of the Mass that they would often memorize the words of the Gospel as they were being proclaimed to them.

We need to remember that in those times most of the people were illiterate except for the clergy and scholars, and printing had not yet been invented. But these early Christians had a faith expectancy so intense that they approached the Liturgy of the Word with a deep love and an urgent desire to absorb everything they could. This helped them better participate in the second part of the Mass, the Liturgy of the Eucharist. The nourishment they received through these two feedings had a remarkable effect by way of miracles and healings in their individual lives and in their life together as a Christian community.

As we saw in the previous chapter, the outpouring of miracles and healings was characteristic of the Church during the first few centuries after the death of Christ. It probably reached its crescendo in the fourth century, when people had a particularly great love for and faith in the Eucharist. Thereafter, people began to attend Mass and receive Communion less devoutly and less frequently. There were various reasons for this decline, but later in the seventeenth century a heretical movement called Jansenism had far-reaching untoward effects on people's attitudes toward the Eucharist. These effects persist in various degrees today.

Jansenism is named after a French bishop, Cornelius Jansen, who wrote a book, *Augustinus*, in 1640 which contained several ideas contrary to the teaching of the Church. Jansen was vigorously opposed by many theologians, and Pope Innocent X condemned the teachings of Jansen in 1654. However, Jansen had his following, and some of his ideas took root in people's thinking. Among other things, Jansen opposed frequent reception of the Eucharist because he felt that human beings were basically unworthy to receive Holy Communion. He taught that only persons with *perfect* contrition could receive the sacraments of penance and Holy Eucharist. Although most of Jansen's teachings eventually fell by the wayside, his influence gradually crept into the laws of the Church. At a certain point, people were permitted to receive Holy Communion only once a month, even though they were required to attend Mass every week.

For a while, this teaching of the Church had a positive effect on people's faith. They would anticipate their monthly Holy Communion with great expectancy and order their whole month around the Sunday when they would be able to receive the Eucharist. For the two weeks before their Communion, they would prepare themselves with intense prayer, mortification, and fasting so they would be worthy to receive Jesus. Communion became the climactic event in their month. The next two weeks were spent in thanksgiving for the graces they had received through the sacrament. This monthly cycle created a high level of expectant faith among many people. Eventually, though, such infrequency in the reception of Jesus in the Eucharist had a detrimental effect on their spiritual lives.

Early in this century, Pope Pius X recognized this inconsistency. To cite a later analogy drawn by Pope Paul VI, attending Mass without receiving Holy Communion was tantamount to having a ring without the diamond in the setting. Attending Mass has value, just as a ring has a certain value. But a ring without the diamond is not as valuable as having a ring with the diamond! As a result, Pope Pius X changed the rules of the Church then in effect and allowed Catholics to receive Communion every day if they so desired.

Diminishing Fervor in the Church Today

Nowadays, it is hard to imagine that anyone would spend two weeks preparing for Communion, or two weeks in thanksgiving afterward. How much we Christians take God for granted today! Consequently, we do not witness the miracles we should. We do not avail ourselves of all the power the sacraments afford.

Granted, today, developing an expectant faith and fervor is not easy. We are living in a toxic atmosphere of secularism, humanism, materialism, and hedonism. We are gradually being poisoned, and almost imperceptibly our faith is becoming enfeebled. It is the gradualism that makes the process so deceiving. The old analogy rings true: You can throw a frog into scalding water and it will jump out immediately, but if you put the frog into lukewarm water and increase the temperature only gradually, the frog will boil to death. Likewise, the gradual erosion of our faith kills us spiritually.

Unfortunately faith among Christians today is diminishing more and more. We only have to look at the statistics. Marriages are collapsing; the divorce rate in the United States has skyrocketed; the institution of the priesthood has been racked by scandal. In the various reported apparitions of the Virgin Mary during this century, she has often spoken of Satan's diabolical plan to destroy marriage, the pillar of society, and the priesthood, the pillar of the Church. This is Satan's plan, his last hurrah. Gradually, we are succumbing to it. We know, by Jesus' promises, that the gates of hell will not prevail against the Church, but they may come close to doing so, especially during the coming time of the great apostasy predicted by Jesus.

This is not the first historical period in which people's faith has been put to the test, and perhaps it is not the last. But times like these are precisely why Jesus put the following question to all his followers: "But when the Son of Man comes, will he find faith on earth?" (Lk 18:8, NAB). In this passage, Jesus is speaking about the point in salvation history when he comes not as Redeemer, as he did the first time, but as Judge.

St. Paul speaks about these times in 1 Timothy 4:1-2 (NAB): "Now the Spirit explicitly says that in the last times some will turn away from the faith by paying attention to deceitful spirits and demonic instructions through the hypocrisy of liars with branded consciences." And he further elaborates on this in 2 Timothy 3:1-9 (NAB):

But understand this: there will be terrifying times in the last days. People will be self-centered and lovers of money, proud, haughty, abusive, disobedient to their parents, ungrateful, irreligious, callous, implacable, slanderous, licentious, brutal, hating what is good, traitors, reckless, conceited, lovers of pleasure rather than lovers of God, as they make a pretense of religion but deny its power. Reject them. For some of these slip into homes and make captives of women weighed down by sins, led by various desires, always trying to learn but never able to reach a knowledge of the truth. Just as Jannes and Jambres opposed Moses, so they also oppose the truth—people of depraved mind, unqualified in the faith. But they will not make further progress, for their foolishness will be plain to all, as it was with those two.

Many things happening in the world today clearly foreshadow St. Paul's scenario for the great apostasy, when the forces of evil become rampant on the earth. At that time some people who *think* they have great faith will leave the Church. At that time people will even abandon the teachings of Sacred Scripture: "Yes, days are coming, says the Lord God, when I will send famine upon the land: Not a famine of bread, or thirst for water, but for hearing the word of the Lord. Then shall they wander from sea to sea and rove from the north to the east in search of the word of the Lord, but they shall not find it"

(Am 8:11-12, NAB). When we come to those times, we will see how little faith there is.

We need to take a good hard look again at Jesus' question, "When the Son of Man comes again, will there be any faith left on earth?" (Lk 18:8). Those who pride themselves on having great faith are the ones who are likely to fall the hardest when the apostasy really comes. They will be disillusioned and confused by all the conflicting teaching from some of the clergy, and from liberal versus conservative *extremes* within the Church. We might be experiencing a foretaste of this right now as we read about battles between the *ultra*-conservatives and the *ultra*-liberals, both of whom are "enemies of the Church" within the Church, as Pope Paul VI said. These factions are causing tremendous conflict, contributing to the loss of many people's faith and gradually destroying the body of Christ. To contravene this, we need stability. We need a source of truth. We need to adhere to Christ, the Bible, and the magisterium of the Church Jesus founded "on this rock" (Mt 16:18)—"the church of the living God, the pillar and foundation of truth" (1 Tm 3:15, NAB).

We need Christ in our hearts; we need the kingdom of God within us. Most of all, we need Christ abiding in us through the Eucharist. We need his corporate presence in the assemblies at the Sacred Liturgy, and we also need a frequent, fervent, personal, intimate contact with Jesus in Holy Communion. The Church has been proclaiming this truth for twenty centuries. If people approached this sacrament intent on availing themselves of all the power it affords, the hemorrhaging of the faith in the Church would stop. Unfortunately, most persons who attend

Mass and who receive Communion are totally unaware of Jesus' presence, both corporately and physically. They might know it theoretically perhaps, but as we have already seen, as many as seventy percent of today's Catholics do not even believe in the real presence of Jesus in the Eucharist. Consequently, because of this ignorance, apathy, and unbelief surrounding the sacrament of the Eucharist, few people obtain the benefits that Jesus makes available.

NINE

Physical Healing From the Eucharist

As we have already seen, there are three major areas in which God's healing action can benefit his creatures. These are in body, soul, and spirit. Let us take a closer look at God's healing action in each of these areas, and the effects we can expect.

The first type of healing flowing from the Eucharist is physical healing.

When I receive a request to give a talk, lead a retreat, or conduct a parish mission, my hosts often suggest the Eucharist as a possible theme. As much as I would like to title my talk simply "The History of the Eucharist" or "The Meaning of the Eucharist," after consulting with my hosts, I usually settle upon "The Healing Power of the Eucharist." Why? Because I know, and they know, that if we use the first two titles, only half as many people will show up. But when the word "healing" is in the title, the turnout is better. It is simply "good box office," so to speak.

I do not fault those people who are drawn by the word "healing" in the title. This is merely an indication of what is really on people's minds and what they really want. They are seeking healing. When I quiz people at these events as to what particular kind of healing they want, most people tell me they want some kind of *physical healing*. Indeed, when we think of healing, we generally think about the body. We want to be healed of migraine headaches, cancer, arthritis, or whatever.

In a certain sense, these people are looking for healing in narrow terms and of the lowest kind. There is nothing wrong with this. Jesus healed many people of their physical ailments during his ministry, and even enticed them to state such requests. For instance, Mark 10:46-52 recounts the healing of Bartimaeus, a blind man: "What do you want me to do for you?" Jesus asked him. "Rabbi, I want to see," he replied. "Go," said Jesus, "your faith has saved you."

Catholics have never lost sight of God's power to heal the physical ailments of his people. Over the centuries Catholics have made pilgrimages to many shrines and sanctuaries renowned for the physical healings that have occurred there. The Marian shrines in Lourdes, France, and in St. Anne de Beaupré, Canada, are two well-known examples. Many people have been healed of physical ailments at both places, and some of the more extraordinary physical healings have been documented by Church authorities and recognized as miracles.

Nevertheless, not all of the hundreds of thousands of people who flock to these shrines each year are necessarily seeking physical healing. Some go as pilgrims who simply want to experience God's presence in their lives—a sort of emotional or spiritual healing. These healings, of course, are not as easy to document as physical healings, but most visitors to these shrines will readily attest to the special graces they received during their visit.

In recent years, the charismatic renewal in the Catholic Church has been instrumental in making Catholics more aware of the Holy Spirit's special "power gift", or charism, of healing. As a result, many people have experienced God's healing power through a variety of means (such as the anointing with oil, the laying on of hands, and intercessory prayer) and in a variety of situations (such as prayer meetings, healing retreats, and healing Masses). These healings include physical, emotional, and spiritual healings.

But for one reason or another, today some Catholics who readily acknowledge the extraordinary ways in which God's healing power has been manifested in places like Lourdes are reticent to acknowledge God's healing power at work in prayer meetings, retreats, and liturgies.

I have celebrated many Masses where people have experienced God's healing power, especially through the Eucharist. Such healings are not necessarily the result of special graces we are experiencing today. Indeed, some amazing testimonies of physical healing, especially as a result of eucharistic devotion, can be found in the annals of Church history. Two such examples are found in a classic work on the Eucharist by Fr. Michael Müller, C.Ss.R., called *The Blessed Eucharist*. Fr. Müller wrote his book in the middle of the nineteenth century.

The first story, dating back to 1824, is that of a woman named Mrs. Ann Mattingly of Washington, D.C. Mrs. Mattingly had been suffering from a dangerous, incurable cancer for seven years and was clearly at death's door. She made a novena in honor of the Most Holy Name of Jesus, and at the end of the novena she received Communion. She knew that the time had come when she would either die or be restored to health, and as she took Communion she uttered the words, "Lord Jesus, thy holy will be glorified!" Her tongue was so rough and parched that she was unable to swallow the host for five or six minutes, but the moment she swallowed it, all pain instantly left her. She was healed immediately. She knelt down and gave thanks to God, and hundreds of visitors streamed into her home for the rest of the day to witness the miracle.

Fr. Müller also recounts the story of a young woman, Ann de Clery, of Metz, France, whose health began to decline at the age of thirteen, and who eventually suffered an incurable paralysis, which was to plague her for almost ten years. She was thin and weak because she was not able to digest food. Throughout the day she suffered from violent headaches and intense pain. Yet, she was totally resigned to God's will for those nine years, and spent her time embroidering altar cloths. A priest brought her Holy Communion every week.

At that point, in the year 1867, an extraordinary event took place. When Ann learned that the Forty Hours Devotion would be celebrated at a nearby church, she insisted on participating. For the first two days, she was not able to attend because of the precarious state of her health. But on the third day, her family carried her there. A nurse held Ann on her knees, though Ann was twenty-three years old. Ann fixed her attention on the Blessed Sacrament and prayed the prayer she would always pray before receiving Holy Communion: "Lord, you can heal me if you so desire." At first a violent pain racked her whole body. Then she felt as though she was penetrated with faith and hope, and became conscious that she was cured. She threw herself on her knees and shouted, "Pray, pray. I am cured!" Ann then rose to her feet and walked out of the church with only the help of her mother's arm. Tears and sobs mingled with the people's prayers.

At home, her mother discovered that the knots Ann had had under her knees had completely disappeared. Later, Ann returned to the church, where she spent forty-five minutes on her knees before the Blessed Sacrament, without feeling the least bit of pain or fatigue. In an instant, she was completely healed. All the ailments that afflicted her disappeared along with the paralysis, and she did not exhibit any of the usual signs of weakness that follow a long illness.

These healing testimonies date from the last century. Jesus was at work then, just as he was when he walked among us, and just as he is today. Furthermore, these healings were not the result of a pilgrimage to any shrine reputed for its healing ministry. These healings were the direct result of a deep faith in the healing power of the Eucharist.

Approaches to Physical Healing

In the realm of physical restoration, doctors practice two primary approaches in medicine: therapeutic medicine (curative) and prophylactic medicine (preventive). Both of these approaches to medicine are instrumental in maintaining good health. Therapeutic medicine treats diseases such as cancer, diabetes, and arthritis in order to restore a person's health, or at least to restore the patient to an optimum state of health.

Prophylactic medicine seeks to prevent disease. Doctors treat many people today for elevated cholesterol and hypertension using both diet and medicines. They know that if no preventive measures are taken and if these conditions are allowed to persist, these people will be at high risk for developing cardiovascular disease and strokes.

Just as doctors use these two approaches to treat their patients, we need to take this two-pronged approach when we pray for healing. Unfortunately, most people wait until they are sick with a disease before they pray for healing. It seldom occurs to them to pray *before* the onset of the disease for prevention or protection against the disease.

Both curative and preventive healing are *maximally* available to us in the Eucharist. We can attend Mass and receive Communion to prevent sickness as well as to heal sickness, but only when the requisite faith is present. This means we can ask the Lord through the Holy Eucharist to protect us from cancer, arthritis, diabetes, back problems, accidental injury, or any one of a myriad of other *physical* diseases or problems.

At the same time, we can ask the Lord to protect us from *emotional* or *spiritual* problem. Married couples should make it a point to pray for a good, strong marriage from their honeymoon on, instead of waiting until a problem has arisen or until their marriage has fallen apart. Peter encourages married couples to be partners in inheriting the precious "gift of life" (1 Pt 3:7), and St. Paul urges them to "submit to one another out of reverence for Christ" (Eph 5:21, NIV). Husbands and wives should be partners together in Christ, praying *together* at home, attending Mass and receiving Communion *together*, while *together* asking Jesus for prevention of any rupture in their marital love. We need the strength of Christ (see Philippians 4:13) in order to avoid future failures. We have to be strengthened to consistently live a life of virtue.

Unlike all the other sacraments, the sacrament of the Eucharist requires that we physically consume the sacred species as food. But as I have noted elsewhere, it is also possible to make a "spiritual communion." Traditionally, spiritual communion is understood as the fervent desire to receive the Eucharist.

This fervent desire should normally precede the reception of the sacrament, and it should express itself in attitudes of faith and love throughout the day after having received Communion. Receiving Communion should never be simply an external or routine action; it must penetrate the heart and mind so that its graces are fully realized in the worshiper.

"Spiritual communion" may also be practiced by those who are unable to approach the Eucharist worthily, or are impeded from so doing, such as those waiting to be received into the Church or those who live in an area where there is no possibility of attending Mass. They can experience a "spiritual communion" by making an act of faith in the real presence of Christ in the Eucharist, together with an intense act of love reaffirming their yearning desire to receive him in the Eucharist. According to St. Alphonsus Liguori, this is a very powerful form of prayer, though it is less effective than physical Communion.

However, most people do have the ability to attend Mass and receive sacramental Communion, thereby availing themselves of the spiritual power of the sacrament. It is important to remember this life-conferring power does not come primarily from the assimilation of the chemically dissolved substance of the eucharistic elements. It comes from the presence of the Divine Person, who remains physically present (until the host is dissolved and no longer has the chemical structure of bread) in our beings for perhaps ten to fifteen minutes. Even when there is no longer the *real physical* presence of Jesus, there remains a *real spiritual* presence of Christ. The material elements, dissolved by our digestive function, are physically assimilated, just as any food is physically assimilated. Spiritually, however, we "assimilate" Christ to a greater or lesser degree, depending on our devotion—namely, how much our faith and love are activated during and after receiving Communion.

Why do I emphasize this spiritual assimilation of the Divine Person of Jesus so much? It is important because Jesus gives us so much through our personal contact with him in the Eucharist. St. Paul speaks about the nine segments of the fruit of the Spirit in Galatians 5:22-23 (NIV): "The fruit of the Spirit is love, joy, peace, patience, kindness, goodness, faithfulness, gentleness, and self-control." St. Thomas Aquinas points out the first three—love, joy, and peace—are the most important. It is precisely these three that are conferred upon us in our physical contact with Jesus in the Eucharist.

In John 15:9, Jesus says, "As the Father has loved me, so have I loved you; abide in *my love*" (RSV, emphasis added). He does not simply say, "Abide in love." In John 15:11 (NAB), he says, "I have told you this so that *my joy* might be in you and your joy might be complete" (emphasis added). He speaks about *his* joy, not merely some joyful emotional experience. In John 14:27, Jesus says, "Peace I leave with you; *my peace* I give to you. Not as the world gives do I give it to you. Do not let your hearts be troubled or afraid" (NAB, emphasis added). Once again he does not say, "I give you peace." He says, "*My peace* I give you." Jesus wants us to experience love, joy, and peace, not as some vague emotions but as genuine fruit of the presence of his Holy Spirit within us. Moreover, he wants the fruit of the Spirit to exercise its multiple function of shaping our patterns of behavior.

The ongoing presence of the Divine Person in our being is proportionate to our faith. In Matthew 8:13, NAB, Jesus said, "...as you have believed, let it be done for you." In Mark 8:22-26, we read the story about a blind man in Bethsaida whom Jesus healed. When Jesus and his disciples arrived in Bethsaida, the people of the village brought a blind man to Jesus and begged Jesus to touch him. Jesus led the blind man outside the village, put spittle on his eyes, and laid his hands on him. Jesus then asked him, "Do you see anything?" The blind man replied, "I see people looking like trees and walking." It was obvious the man could not see clearly; it was as though he still had cataracts on his eyes and could see only vaguely. Jesus had worked a miracle, but it was not complete. Jesus then laid his hands on him a second time. This time the man's sight was completely restored.

Why was he not completely healed the first time? Mark does not give us a reason. But Mark tells us that the townspeople brought the blind man to Jesus so he would touch him. This is a different scenario from the other accounts of healing where the ailing persons themselves would cry out to Jesus so he would touch them and heal them. We might speculate, therefore, that the blind man was not entirely receptive to being healed and thus lacked, at first, the faith needed to be totally healed. Might this explain why it was a two-step healing?

Whatever the case, both the element of receptivity and the question of faith are important. Jesus said, "...as you have believed, let it be done for you" (Mt 8:13, NAB). He did not say, "Let it be done for you according to my divine power." There is nothing missing, of course, in Jesus' divine power. But people do have limited degrees of faith and, consequently, experience limited degrees of healing.

Concomitantly, people have limited degrees of love, and this too can determine whether a person will experience God's healing action in his or her life. Sometimes people want healing just for selfish reasons: they do not want to be healed to give glory to God but to be free from pain. They pray selfishly, asking with wrong motives. As St. James says, "You ask but do not receive, because you ask wrongly, to spend it on your passions" (Jas 4:3, NAB). They are not interceding for good health in order to be able to work more effectively for the Lord. They just want freedom from pain. These people are focused on themselves. God loves them with all their limitations and works with them where they are. Nonetheless, their selfish motives are limiting Jesus' healing power in them.

The Ultimate Healing That Awaits Us

As we have already seen, health-restoring vitality is available through the mutual union of Holy Communion. At the same time, Jesus promises us the most perfect form of healing through the Eucharist with the words, "Whoever eats my flesh and drinks my blood has eternal life, and *I will raise him on the last day*" (Jn 6:54, NAB, emphasis added).

What exactly will happen on that last day? When Jesus comes again, the dead will rise: "For the Lord himself, with a word of command, with the voice of an archangel and with the trumpet of God, will come down from heaven, and the dead in Christ will rise first" (1 Thes 4:16, NAB). Those who are alive when Jesus comes again will experience the rapture: "Then we who are alive, who are left, will be caught up together with them in the clouds to meet the Lord in the air. Thus we will always be with the Lord" (1 Thes 4:17, NAB).

In one sense, the most perfect form of healing is death. When it is time for us to go, death acts as a healing because it frees us from pain and suffering. For this reason, we should be thankful for death. Still, for the faith-filled person, there is a healing beyond death that is even better than death, namely the resurrection of the body. As we read in John 5:28-29 (NAB): "Do not be amazed at this, because the hour is coming in which all who are in the tombs will hear his voice and will come out, those who have done good deeds to the resurrection of life, but those who have done wicked deeds to the resurrection of condemnation."

At the time of the second coming of Christ, the disembodied souls of the just, who are already enjoying the presence of God in heaven, will be joined with their newly glorified bodies now resurrected to full life, and the souls of the reprobate, suffering in hell, will be joined with their bodies. The bodies and souls of the just will revel in eternal glory, while the bodies and souls of the reprobate will suffer eternal damnation.

Thus, the resurrection of the body for those who are saved offers the ultimate, most perfect form of healing. And this amazing and supreme form of healing by way of the resurrection and glorification of the bodies of just persons is what Jesus promises to those who receive his own glorified body in Holy Communion: "I will raise him on the last day."

As St. Thomas Aquinas pointed out, all other healings are implicitly contained in this ultimate healing that will occur at the time of the resurrection of the body. At that time, our bodies will be just like Jesus' glorified body. In Philippians 3:20-21 (NAB), St. Paul assures us: "But our citizenship is in heaven, and from it we also await a savior, the Lord Jesus Christ. He will change our lowly body to conform with his glorified body by the power that enables him also to bring all things into subjection to himself."

Elsewhere St. Paul elaborates on the changes that await us: "So also is the resurrection of the dead. It is sown corruptible; it is raised incorruptible. It is sown dishonorable; it is raised glorious. It is sown weak; it is raised powerful. It is sown a natural body; it is raised a spiritual body. If there is a natural body, there is also a spiritual one" (1 Cor 15:42-44, NAB). This is the *highest and ultimate form of healing*, and Jesus speaks of it in the context of reward for receiving him in Communion.

What will our glorified bodies be like? In St. Paul's descriptions in various passages of what awaits the redeemed, four essential qualities of the resurrected body seem to emerge: agility, clarity, subtlety, and impassability.

Agility is the ability to move with the speed of thought. One form of this is the rapture: "Then we who are alive, who are left, will be caught up together with them in the clouds to meet the Lord in the air. Thus we shall always be with the Lord. Therefore, console one another with these words" (1 Thes 4:17-18, NAB). We will be able to move immediately anywhere we want: "In the time of their visitation they shall shine, and shall dart about as sparks through stubble" (Wis 3:7, NAB). If we want to see the far side of the moon, we just have to think about it and we are there. Jesus manifested this quality when he moved throughout the Holy Land (see Matthew 18:7-10 and Luke 24:31) in the few days after his resurrection with his glorified body, meeting with his apostles here and there, and at his ascension (see Acts 1:9).

Clarity means brilliance, effulgence, beauty, and radiance, as Jesus manifested in his transfiguration. Matthew 17:2 tells us that Jesus "was transfigured before them; his face shone like the sun and his clothes became white as light." Mark 9:3 describes the transfiguration of Jesus in this way: "And his clothes became dazzling white, such as no fuller on earth could bleach them." Our bodies will be fantastically beautiful.

Subtlety means that our bodies will truly be physical bodies, but they will act in a spiritual manner. Just as Jesus in his glorified body walked into the Upper Room through locked doors (see John 20:19), we will be able to walk through walls. With our glorified body, if someone gets in our way, we will be able to walk right through them instead of walking around them!

Impassability refers to the inability to suffer pain or to suffer from defects. We will be totally free from wrinkles, bulges, pain, fatigue, grief, anguish, and depression. St. John reminds us, "They will not hunger or thirst anymore, nor will the sun or any heat strike them. For the Lamb who is in the center of the throne will shepherd them and lead them to springs of life-giving water, and God will wipe away every tear from their eyes" (Rv 7:16-17). Later he assures us, "He will wipe every tear from their eyes, and there shall be no more death or mourning, wailing or pain, for the old order has passed away" (Rv 21:4, NAB).

Indeed, this is true healing! When Jesus draws a parallel between his resurrection and our own resurrected bodies, he does so in the context of the Eucharist. Why did he make this close connection between the Eucharist and this ultimate healing that awaits us? The reason is simple. It is the *glorified* body of Christ that we receive in the Eucharist. The degree to which we have eucharistic devotion and practice is the degree to which we will have healing, not only in this life but also in the next life, when the fullest degree of healing awaits us. Do we ever think of that when we receive Communion?

As we participate more and more faithfully in the Eucharist, we can anticipate a future having bodies full of vitality, health, strength, and immunity. Our physical bodies, when nourished by Jesus' own body in eucharistic form, will be the fulfillment of Jesus' own promise that those who eat his Body and drink his Blood will have their own bodies raised on the last day (see John 6:53-54).

Emotional Healing From the Eucharist

The second kind of healing that awaits us in the Eucharist is emotional healing, a healing that occurs in our minds. We have already seen that the fruit of the Spirit—especially love, joy, and peace—are available to us through our contact with Jesus in the Eucharist and provide us with healing beyond the mere physical. In fact, both spiritual and emotional healings ensue when we receive Jesus in Holy Communion.

It is important to note that healing us emotionally was a part of Christ's purpose in coming to us on earth. In Luke 4:16-30, Jesus was in Nazareth and went to the synagogue to pray on the Sabbath day. He stood up to read and was handed a scroll of the prophet Isaiah; he unrolled it and read this passage: "The Spirit of the Lord is upon me, because he has anointed me to bring glad tidings to the poor. He has sent me to proclaim liberty to captives and recovery of sight to the blind, to let the oppressed go free, and to proclaim a year acceptable to the Lord.... Today this scripture passage is fulfilled in your hearing" (Lk 4:18-21, NAB).

The passage to which Jesus refers is Isaiah 61:1-2. There, the original reads, "He has sent me to bring glad tidings to the lowly, *to heal the brokenhearted*" (emphasis added). Besides being sent to heal people physically, Jesus reiterates here that he has also been sent to heal the brokenhearted—those who are depressed, sorrowful, or unhappy—as well as to release those who are in bondage, particularly bondage to evil spirits. Jesus' compassion covered the whole gamut of human dysfunctions, whether physical, emotional, or spiritual.

When we are in intimate contact with Jesus physically present in the Eucharist and are completely open to assimilating the continued spiritual presence of Christ, we are maximally disposed for every type of healing. In calling to mind the benefits of receiving the Holy Eucharist, St. Thomas Aquinas declared that it is the most health-giving of all the sacraments: by it sins are washed away, virtues are increased, and the soul is fed and filled with an abundance of all spiritual gifts. The Eucharist is truly a banquet of spiritual delights! Sadly, though, many Catholics today are ignorant of the subtle yet powerful ways in which these health-giving effects of the Eucharist are at work when we receive this sacrament.

Our spiritual union with Jesus in the Eucharist is an intimate union. If we approach the Eucharist with the right predisposition, the soul of Christ will be united with our souls to make us of one heart and one mind with him. We will be caught up in God's wondrous benefits, enthralled by his rapturous beauty, aware of his holiness and righteousness, and overwhelmed by his inexhaustible goodness. When we receive the Eucharist devoutly, the mind of Christ will enlighten our minds with the radiance of faith and help us recognize the gospel truths, which are often clouded over and obscured by our natural instincts. Like the two disciples on their way to Emmaus, we too will experience a special closeness with the risen Jesus and, like them, exclaim, "Were not our hearts burning [within us] while he spoke with us on the way and opened the scriptures to us?" (Lk 24:32, NAB). Only when Jesus repeated the Last Supper ritual of consecrating the bread did the two recognize his august presence. At that point, "their eyes were opened" (Lk 24:31, NAB) and they were healed of their despondency.

Our spiritual union with Jesus in the Eucharist will always transform us. Little by little, our thoughts, ideas, convictions, and feelings will undergo a change. We will no longer judge everything by the world's standards but by the standards of the gospels. The Eucharist is the most excellent aid in prompting us to ask ourselves the question so popular among young people today, especially those who have given their lives over to Jesus: "What would Jesus do?" As a result, our desires will also undergo a change. We will realize that our desires are so often wrong. Our frequent reception of the Eucharist will strengthen us so that our ambitions, desires, and choices conform to those of Christ, whom we are receiving.

Finally, as we experience changes in our desires, we will also experience a real change of heart. We will be set free from our more or less conscious self-centeredness and from our lower natural inclinations and attachments so that we might love God and our neighbor more ardently, more generously, and even more passionately. We will be able to join our voices to that of St. Paul, who in his spiritual transformation exclaimed, "Yet I live, no longer I, but Christ lives in me" (Gal 2:20, NAB).

We must never underestimate the degree to which different virtues will be strengthened through our reception of the Eucharist and the healing effect these virtues will ultimately have on our emotional well-being. For example, the Eucharist generates strength. In fact, long ago Holy Communion was called "the bread of the strong." The grind of daily life may often overtax our energy to the point that we find ourselves bending from the strain. Yet Jesus comes to us in the Eucharist with his mighty grace and energizes us, renews us, and strengthens us, enabling us to take up our cross daily and follow him.

At times we may feel as though we are strong yet lack the courage to face the ever-recurring drudgery of a home life or work life that is the result of misunderstanding, want, or illness. When we feel emotionally drained like this, the Eucharist can generate greater courage in us. When we find ourselves losing heart, the best thing to do is to make contact with Jesus and draw courage from him in Holy Communion so we can get back on our feet. He is there for us.

The Eucharist can also help us grow in patience. We might exhibit tremendous strength and courage when confronted with tremendous ordeals, yet still notice a lack of patience when confronted with the minute trials that come our way, whether it be the family member who squeezes the toothpaste in the middle or the coworker who habitually greets us with a whack on the back. But when we receive Jesus in Holy Communion and realize what a tremendous privilege it is to be united with him, we see these silly trials for what they are. Jesus will supply us with the grace to retrain ourselves and even with the ability to overlook, or forgive and forget, these petty irritants. In addition, the increase of God's love in us that follows a good Communion will bring us closer to God and to others.

These are only a few examples of the changes that occur when we receive the Eucharist *devoutly*. We should always desire these changes and take an active role in seeking them out. The benefits may seem imperceptible at first, but gradually they will have a powerful effect on our spiritual and emotional health. At the same time, we should also take great care to leave the door open for Jesus to heal our emotional wounds in sudden and dramatic ways.

Many people have shared with me their stories of how Jesus in the Eucharist has healed deep-rooted, emotional wounds in some unexpected yet lasting ways. Often people are hesitant to share these healings because it is more difficult to authenticate emotional healings than it is to substantiate physical healings. Physical wounds are visible to the eye; emotional wounds are not.

Recently I received a letter from a woman who experienced an emotional healing through the Eucharist. She had become pregnant when she was young and unmarried, so her parents made her get an abortion. In a letter to me, she related how God worked in her life:

"After the abortion, I couldn't live with myself for what I had done, and became emotionally distraught. My mother tried to console me by reminding me of that old axiom, 'Time heals all wounds,' but there was never a day that went by after that when I didn't think of the baby who had once been inside my womb.

"Years passed and I happened to see a young woman on Christian television who had also had an abortion, telling the audience to give their aborted babies a name, and assuring us that our babies were in heaven. I took her advice and named my baby 'Elizabeth,' for I always felt the infant in my womb was a girl. As for her stating that the babies were in heaven and not just in limbo or nonexistent, I wasn't sure if she knew what she was talking about, but could only hope.

"Many years went by before I attended one of your seminars on Healing the Family Tree. The seminar was wonderful, and I put my baby's name and her father's name on my family tree to be prayed for at the altar during Mass, as you suggested.

"It wasn't until the seminar was nearly over, however, and before you were about to distribute Holy Communion, that you stated that many miracles had been reported to you by participants in the seminars when they received Holy Communion. I thought to myself, somewhat sarcastically, 'No miracles ever happen to me.'

"Well, I received Communion and returned to my seat with the host in my mouth. As soon as I sat down, and with my eyes closed, I had a vision. I saw my daughter in heaven wearing a light brown dress with puffy sleeves. She wasn't an infant or twenty-two years old, which would have been her natural age if she had lived, but she was a little girl of about ten years of age. Jesus stood next to her with his arm around her shoulders. They both stood beaming with an indescribable joy, and waving their hands vigorously at me as if to say that everything was all right. It was a heavenly joy, so radiantly pure and wonderful that words cannot adequately describe it.

"From that day on, I knew my child was safe in the arms of Jesus, living in complete happiness and joy in paradise."

ELEVEN

Spiritual Healings From the Eucharist

The third kind of healing that awaits us in the Eucharist is spiritual healing. Jesus has promised his true believers an eternal banquet, inviting them to "eat and drink at my table in my kingdom" (Lk 22:30, NAB). As a foretaste of that eternal banquet, he invites us in this life to the eucharistic table, where, as the hymn phrases it, "God and man at table have sat down."

This banquet has its origins, of course, in Jesus' last meal with his disciples, the Passover meal. This was the first Mass. It was a transition from the old covenant to the new covenant, from the old dispensation to the new dispensation, from the Old Testament to the New Testament. "This cup is the *new covenant* in my blood, which will be shed for you," Jesus said (Lk 22:20, NAB). These are the sacred words repeated today at the consecration of the wine each time we celebrate the Holy Sacrifice of the Mass. This covenant is available to us now in this continually renewed pledge of that future heavenly banquet.

The Passover meal was a commemorative meal in memory of the Exodus, when Moses led the Israelites out of Egypt and freed them from the slavery they had endured there. Jesus and his disciples ate this meal on Holy Thursday, only a few hours before Jesus was to be crucified on Calvary. With this meal, he was forewarning his disciples he was going to shed his blood, thereby becoming their new Redeemer, or Rescuer. He was telling them that this Passover meal, the Last Supper, was a transition point. No longer would they celebrate it in memory of Moses and what the Lord had done for his people at that time. He was starting something new: By his redemptive act on Calvary, Jesus, the new Moses, would lead his people out of slavery—not slavery to the Egyptians but slavery to the devil. In one meal, he overlapped the old dispensation with the new dispensation. Furthermore, he did not come to destroy the old covenant; he came to fulfill it (see Matthew 5:17).

This concept of covenant is very important. A covenant is not the same thing as a contract; a covenant is open-ended. Covenants were often ratified with a meal in the ancient Near East, and it is enlightening to look at this custom in its historical context. In the culture of that time, a meal was the expression of a bond of friendship. When you shared food with someone, you were pledging your protection to that person.

A true story about a Persian nobleman illustrates this Near Eastern concept of covenant relationship. This Persian nobleman was walking in his garden when a man climbed over the wall of the garden and approached him. He was fleeing a lynch mob bent on killing him. The nobleman, who had authority to grant amnesty, had pity on this man because he was going to be slaughtered. The nobleman was eating a peach at the time, so he broke off part of the peach and shared it with the man. When the clamoring mob finally came into the garden to pursue this man, the nobleman said, "What did he do?" The people replied, "He just committed a murder and the murder victim was your son." The man was brokenhearted to learn that his son had been killed and that the culprit was the man with whom he had just shared his peach. But he said, "I've shared food with you. I am covenanted with you. We've shared food together, so you are free to live. Go in peace."

In a sense, we have all killed God's Son on Calvary. Jesus died because of us, because of our sins. Yet, we are protected from any culpability because of the covenant promise concluded by the sharing of food—the consecrated bread and wine, Jesus' Body that has been broken and his Blood that has been shed so that our sins may be forgiven.

In the Holy Sacrifice of the Mass, we do not repeat Calvary; we reenact Calvary. Hebrews 9:27-28 tells us that Christ died once for our sins and that he can die no more. Christ does not die a physical death on the altar; he undergoes a mystical or symbolic death. It is an unbloody sacrifice that is "reenacted" on stage, so to speak. However, even though the death of Christ on the altar *is not real*, the presence of Christ on the altar after the consecration *is real*. This is an important distinction in eucharistic theology that most non-Catholics do not understand and most Catholics, unfortunately, do not believe. The death of Christ on the altar is not real, but the person of Christ after the consecration is real. Because the consecration is not just a human act but a God-man (theandric) act, Christ's "mystical" death in the Mass can produce the same effect as if he were dying on Calvary.

St. Paul gives further meaning to this symbolic or eucharisticized death of the present and life-giving Christ on the altar: "For as often as you eat this bread and drink the cup, you proclaim the *death* of the Lord until he comes" (1 Cor 11:26, NAB, emphasis added). It is in Jesus' death, reenacted on the altar, that we have the Eucharist. It is here that we have its healing focus.

Deliverance From Intrinsic Evil

When Jesus reenacts the sacrifice of Calvary during the Holy Sacrifice of the Mass, he is, in effect, opening to us his Sacred Heart in a flood of healing. Isaiah 53:4-5 (NAB) tells us: "Yet it was our infirmities that he bore, our sufferings that he endured, while we thought of him as stricken, as one smitten by God and afflicted. But he was pierced for our offenses, crushed for our sins, upon him was the chastisement that makes us whole, by his stripes we were healed." Similarly, 1 Peter 2:24 (NAB) says, "He himself bore our sins in his body upon the cross, so that, *free from sin, we might live for righteousness. By his wounds you have been healed*" (emphasis added). Thus, Jesus' death brought spiritual healing from the ravages of sin, and still does so today by his ever-repeated eucharistic sacrifice. Matthew quotes that passage from Isaiah in reference to both spiritual and physical healing: "He drove out the spirits by a word and cured *all* the sick" (Mt 8:16, emphasis added).

Thus, three times Scripture assures us that, because of Jesus' suffering and death on the cross, our pain, oppression, spiritual sickness (sin), and even demonic contamination are lifted. By

Jesus' passion and death, we can claim all four types of healing, discussed in a previous chapter: physical, emotional, spiritual (intrinsic), and deliverance (extrinsic) healing. We only need to appropriate this healing through faith.

Unfortunately, few people have the faith to say, for example, "I don't have to suffer this headache, Lord. You've suffered it already for me with a crown of thorns." If we did have the intense faith to believe that "by his wounds you have been healed," especially when we are reenacting the covenanted suffering and death of Christ symbolically in the Eucharist, then we would truly grasp the healing process that can occur in Communion. We would truly understand the covenant words of the nobleman to his son's murderer: "We've shared food together in this covenant, so you are free to live. Go in peace." We would realize that we are protected, and that protection is also preventive healing: protection from accidents, protection from disease, and protection from disorder, until it is time for us to finish our lives and go to heaven. As St. Paul reminds us, "How much more then, since we are now justified by his blood, will we be saved through him from the wrath. Indeed, if, while we were enemies, we were reconciled to God through the *death* of his Son, how much more, once reconciled, will we be saved by his *life*" (Rom 5:9-10, NAB, emphasis added).

Of course, other spiritual healings occur in the Eucharist. One form of spiritual healing is that we come to recognize Jesus in many hidden forms. Jesus accompanied his disciples on the road to Emmaus for quite a distance, yet they failed to recognize him. In fact, their whole conversation revolved around Jesus of Nazareth and all the events that had taken place in

Jerusalem a few days before. Finally, as they approached the village and night was beginning to fall, they urged this stranger to stay with them for the night. When they sat down to eat, this stranger "took bread, said the blessing, broke it, and gave it to them" (Lk 24:30, NAB). It was only at this point that they recognized him. Through the Eucharist, we too come to recognize (by faith) Christ in his hidden forms.

Before this "healing," Jesus might be for us the "hidden" Christ, such as the besotten skid row derelict lying in the gutter or any other person in whom the presence of Jesus is difficult to recognize. "If you have done it to one of these, you have done it to me." In this eucharistically induced "recognition healing," we find and come to recognize the hidden Christ all around us. Then we begin to notice that our interpersonal relationships are enhanced because we have found Jesus in his many hidden forms just as the disciples on the road to Emmaus found him in the eucharistic banquet he provided for them before he disappeared from their sight.

Deliverance From Extrinsic Evil

Spiritual healing can also take the form of "deliverance," not just from intrinsic evil (sin) but also from extrinsic evil (demonic interference). In our prayers we ask God not only to "forgive us our trespasses" but also to "deliver us from evil." This latter petition is a request for another type of spiritual healing provided by the Eucharist, namely spiritual power over the enemy and protection from his wiles. Those who receive Communion devoutly and fervently are not only healed of the effects of sin in their lives but also protected from the attacks of demonic forces. Scripture tells us, "You cannot have a part in both the Lord's table and the table of demons" (1 Cor 10:21, NIV).

The enemy—the thief, as Jesus calls him—tries to "steal, destroy and kill." He is essentially anti-life and can be subdued only by the divine Life-Giver, who said in contrast, "I came so that they might have *life* and have it more abundantly" (Jn 10:10, emphasis added). "Indeed," St. John records, "the Son of God was revealed to destroy the works of the devil" (1 Jn 3:8). This "exorcistic" mission of Jesus was his premiere healing ministry, performed in many ways and instances (and even at a distance when faith was intense, as recorded in Mark 7:29-30). But it would seem that Jesus' deliverance healing is even more accessible to us when he is allowed to exercise this ministry by his presence in Holy Communion, as we abide in him and he in us (see John 6:56, RSV).

The ancient prayer *Anima Christi* is often used exorcistically, especially with the phrase, "In thy wounds hide me." That is where the devil dares not come, for he dreads the precious blood spilled from those wounds. Christ, the "wounded healer" (who was "wounded for our iniquities," that is, for our capitulations to the enemy), uses those wounds to dispel the evil one, for they are permanent signs that Jesus is the conquering Redeemer. It is "by his wounds we are healed" (Is 53:5).

The precious blood from the wounds of Jesus is offered to us at Communion (present in one or both species, by host or by cup), while that same precious blood is offered to the Eternal Father in atonement for sins that have wounded our souls. In the eucharistic context, praying the Our Father elicits great power for deliverance healing: "Deliver us from evil." Only divine ingenuity could devise such intimacy in which to exercise Jesus' messianic ministry of "destroying the works of the devil."

We already know that the first Mass was the occasion of a Passover meal. The word "Passover," as explained in Exodus 12:27, is derived from the fact that the Israelites were "passed over" by the angel of death; this happened only because the *blood* of the sacrificial lamb was placed on the doorposts of their homes (see Exodus 12:23). But St. John reminds us that our own deliverance is also by the blood of the Sacrificial Lamb— Jesus himself (see Revelation 7:14). "Christ, our Passover lamb, has been sacrificed" (1 Cor 5:7), we say in the Mass, where he is symbolically sacrificed again and again as we "proclaim the Lord's death until he comes" (1 Cor 11:26, NIV). The Eucharist makes the blood of the Sacrificial Lamb present to us today, and its power for deliverance healing is far greater than that of the lamb's blood on the Israelites' door lintels. When the Eucharist is devoutly received, this deliverance healing can scatter the evil spirits of lust, infirmity, divorce, depression, fear, and sloth and countless other forms of evil entities that constantly assail us.

One of the most dramatic forms of spiritual healing through the Eucharist is the popular practice of healing the family tree through offering a Mass for the living and deceased persons in one's family. I discuss this practice at length in my book, *Healing Your Family Tree*. Scripture in several places tells us, "The sins of the parents are visited upon the children to the third and fourth generation." The sins of our ancestors affect us; and our sins, in turn, affect our offspring. The Eucharist is the most powerful means of breaking this bondage. Many healings have been reported by people who have had a Mass offered for their family tree, attended it, and asked the Lord at the consecration and at Holy Communion to cover them and their family with his precious blood to purify the "bad blood" (a biblical term for any transgenerational bondage). By God's mercy, especially in the Eucharist, family trees have been spiritually healed.

TWELVE

Our Holy Privilege

Most Catholics today have heard about the Shroud of Turin and are somewhat acquainted with its long and controversial history. The Shroud of Turin is a brown linen cloth about fourteen feet long and three-and-a-half feet wide that bears the imprint of a human body. For centuries many Christians have believed the image on the shroud is that of Jesus and have venerated it as the fine linen in which the body of Christ was wrapped for burial. It is an amazing relic that has baffled scientists for centuries. In fact, scientists today are still at a loss to explain how the image was produced.

Every public display of the Shroud of Turin generates great excitement, as well as a constant stream of pilgrims. Travel agencies charter additional planes and buses, and book every available hotel bed in the city in order to respond to the demand. When the Shroud was put on public display for six weeks in 1978, 3.5 million people traveled to Turin for a glimpse of this venerable relic. In 1998, the Shroud of Turin was once again put on public display for six weeks, and almost 2.5 million people (including Pope John Paul II) made a point to see it. In fact, you might even know someone who traveled halfway around the world to venerate this relic of our Savior; perhaps you even experienced a holy envy and wished you could have gone too.

If so, you must never lose sight of the fact that, however poor and insignificant your parish church might seem, you will find something even greater there—the living *person* of Jesus Christ, willing not merely to be adored as God but also to enter into the most intimate communion with you. His body is far more sacred than the shroud that enswathed it. "Is not the body more important than clothes?" Jesus asked his followers (Mt 6:25, NIV). Have you been indifferent to Jesus' living presence in the tabernacle in your local parish church? Likewise, if you have a holy envy of the apostles who were present at the first Mass, the Last Supper, remember that you too can enjoy that same privilege each time you attend Mass. If you have a holy envy of the woman who was healed by merely touching the hem of Jesus' garment, remember that you too can touch Jesus anytime by receiving him in Holy Communion. If you have a holy envy of the shepherds who came to the crib at Bethlehem and who probably took turns hugging the Divine Infant in their arms, remember that you too can embrace Jesus in Holy Communion.

You may wish, at times, that you could have experienced the wondering adoration of the Magi when they visited the child Jesus: You too may have that same experience when you adore Jesus in the Blessed Sacrament. Perhaps you have even pondered upon how Mary felt as she bore Jesus in her womb: You too can experience that same privilege when you have Jesus living within you after Communion. All these privileges are, in some way, yours when you receive the same Jesus, not just within your arms but within your very body in Holy Communion.

Remember, though, you can enhance this privilege in two ways. First of all, enjoy this privilege often. Secondly, enjoy this privilege to the fullest, with the greatest fervor. Theologians have two terms that help us understand this. The first, *ex opere operato*, describes how we receive grace by virtue of the act itself. Each time we receive Jesus worthily in Holy Communion, we receive grace just by doing so, regardless of how we might be feeling or how strong our faith may be at the time. For this reason, we should enjoy the privilege of receiving Jesus in the Eucharist as often as possible. The other term, *ex opere operantis*, describes how we determine the amount of grace we receive by virtue of our disposition when we receive Jesus in Holy Communion. This refers to the quality of the devotion with which we receive him. The more devoutly we receive Jesus in the Eucharist, the more grace we receive.

Thus, two people can receive Communion at the same time, but it is theoretically possible for one to receive thousands of times more grace than the other by simply having a little more love for Jesus in the sacrament of love. We have a "fingertip control" over the amount of grace we receive in the sacrament. Every communicant free of serious sin will receive some grace; some will receive much more than others because of their fervor. Correspondingly, we also have a "fingertip control" over the *amount of healing* we receive. Everyone will receive a little healing in some way, but some will receive truly astonishing healings. The grace received, depending on one's subjective disposition, is grace that flows *ex opere operantis*. The most significant "dispositions" are faith and love in the recipient—a "faith expressing itself through love" (Gal 5:6, NIV).

"Will there be any faith left when the Son of Man comes again?" (Lk 18:8). The times will be so evil, "the love of most will grow cold" (Mt 24:12, NIV). We are living in those faithless, loveless times. Let us receive Jesus in the Eucharist *frequently*, and let us receive Jesus in the Eucharist *devoutly*. If we keep these two basic goals in mind, we will be maximally disposed for receiving God's love, God's grace, and God's benefits in the awesome sacrament of the Eucharist. Viewed from our future position in heaven, we will recognize that "from the fullness of his grace we have all received one blessing after another" (Jn 1:16, NIV).